A Year in the Life of an Excellent Elementary School

HOW TO ORDER THIS BOOK

BY PHONE: 800-233-9936 or 717-291-5609, 8AM-5PM Eastern Time

BY FAX: 717-295-4538

BY MAIL: Order Department
Technomic Publishing Company, Inc.
851 New Holland Avenue, Box 3535
Lancaster, PA 17604, U.S.A.

BY CREDIT CARD: American Express, VISA, MasterCard

A Year in the Life of the Life of an Excellent Elementary School

Lessons Derived from Success

EDWARD A. WYNNE

PHOTOGRAPHS BY EDWARD A. WYNNE AND STEVE KAGAN

TECHNOMIC
PUBLISHING CO., INC.
LANCASTER · BASEL

A Year in the Life of an Excellent Elementary School
a TECHNOMIC®publication

Published in the Western Hemisphere by
Technomic Publishing Company, Inc.
851 New Holland Avenue
Box 3535
Lancaster, Pennsylvania 17604 U.S.A.

Distributed in the Rest of the World by
Technomic Publishing AG

Photos credited to Edward A. Wynne, except numbers 3, 6, 15, 30,
38, 39, 44, 45, 46, 48, 54, 75, 76, 80, 90, 91, 113, 120, 121, 123,
124, 125, 127, and 128 are credited to Steve Kagan.

Printed in the United States of America
10 9 8 7 6 5 4 3 2

Main entry under title:
  A Year in the Life of an Excellent Elementary School: Lessons Derived from Success

A Technomic Publishing Company book
Bibliography: p.

Library of Congress Card No. 92-56466
ISBN No. 0-87762-963-3

*To Rosemary Culverwell, and the many other committed principals
and teachers whose visions have helped our children*

THIS book is definitely not the product of an academic toiling away in some lonely attic or library carrel. It was born through engagement with vital events, and thanks to the kindness and support provided to me by a number of divergent people and institutions.

First, I needed financing to pay for photographic help, advice, equipment, and developing services. A generous gift from Noel and Michele Moore supplied the necessary resources.

Next, I needed an elementary school—and its staff and community—willing to tolerate my planned hundred days of probing, watching, photographing, and being a general busybody—without any guarantees about what the final product would say. Then, I needed to obtain formal permission to do my study from the school board or other governing agency. In the school I had to find a small group of teachers, administrators, parents, and students who would make themselves especially available to my prying ears and eyes. Next, I needed to find and employ a skilled and tactful free-lance photographer, to supplement some of my own photography, and counsel me on how to handle the photographic challenges posed by the project. Finally, I needed some tolerant, patient, and wise human being to encourage me during the inevitable frustrations accompanying such an elaborate project.

And so, once I had financing, after some complex searching I found: the Frank W. Reilly Elementary School in the Chicago public school system. Its faculty and community agreed to cooperate with my study. Thanks to the counsel of Carole Perlman, I received formal permission from the Chicago Board of Education to work in the school. Then, in the school, I found my principal, Rosemary Culverwell and her assistant, Jayne Swiatek; and next, my teachers (and their classes): Helen Estes, Gloria Windham, Elizabeth Lucas, Bernice Humphery, and Patricia Canepa.

At a later stage, I came to know Pamela Kane, the Reilly PTA president, who generously supplied me with precious labor in organizing my photographs. With these key figures came a diverse assortment of faculty, pupils, and parents, who advised, supported, and tolerated me in an endless variety of ways. Next, I discovered Steve Kagan, whose patient and acute advice made my photographic efforts possible. Finally, as on many past occasions, for encouragement I turned to my harassed and tolerant wife, Judy. As in the past, she once again backed me when I needed it, and cared enough to prod me, too, when I deserved that.

It's been a wonderful year in my life. Thank you all very, very much. I hope I have been accurate and fair, and that this project helps some children.

Chapter One

INTRODUCTION

THIS book portrays, with photographs and prose, a year in the life of an excellent elementary school, as one might describe a year in the life of a farm, family, hospital, or other institution. The "year in the life of" approach is a useful way of describing a school, because a school is an enterprise with an essentially cyclic program.

The description includes interpretative comments on the policies and practices that make the school excellent. From the description and comments, educators (and even interested laypersons) can discover ways to improve their own local schools and classrooms. Furthermore, the Schema in the Appendix provides readers with a carefully detailed outline—partly derived from this study—useful for analyzing or reorganizing an existing school.

The study focuses on the Reilly school. Reilly is a real, relatively typical—but very well run—Chicago public school, serving a lower income neighborhood. I visited the school over 100 times during a recent school year, and closely followed many of its basic activities. During this year, the school did not have any extraordinary economic help or other unusual resources, except for able leadership and a good staff.

As readers will see, many of the policies applied in Reilly might be characterized as relatively "old fashioned." Students were expected to apply themselves to learning. Teachers worked hard at instruction. Good discipline and character development were priority matters. And time was set aside for responsible fun and spectacle. Why and whether such policies were finally effective in Reilly is partly up to the judgments of you, the readers.

INHERENTLY INTERESTING

Many readers will find the photographs and narrative inherently interesting. The people and situations involved are complex and often heartwarming. In general, the school is an upbeat place. Its staff is comprised largely of dedicated, good-spirited, and competent people, who are successful in their difficult and important work. Following the advice of Oliver Cromwell, the photographs present their subjects "as they are, warts and all." They vividly portray the participants' immediate emotions, as revealed in their postures, facial expressions, and gestures. The photos enable readers to form their own opinions of complex events, rather than having to rely on the author's descriptions.

The precise information photos can supply is especially important in any effort—such as this book—aiming to foster school improvement. Many studies have concluded that educators will try proposed innovations only if they see practices in operation in realistic settings. In the New Testament story of doubting Thomas, the apostle Thomas refused to believe Christ had risen unless he actually touched the wounds in Christ's hands and side. The story recites a psychological truth: Thomas, like most emotionally healthy people, hesitated to believe information that would entirely change his life unless he felt the basic evidence with his own hands. Similarly, educators are reluctant to carry out ambitious changes unless they see and hear such innovations in operation in typical school sites. The educators (quite properly) mistrust the accuracy of reports and interpretations written by persons already deeply sympathetic to particular innovations. Unfortunately, no book can physically take educators to visit remote school sites where unusual policies are being applied. However, photos can be the next best thing: they can show us the emotions and conduct of the pupils and educators engaged in the recommended practices.

Present and potential educators will feel encouraged by knowing about Reilly and its faculty's activities. Such knowledge ennobles their work, and adds to their professional skills. Even noneducators can understand the challenges confronting the Reilly people, and identify with their strivings and achievements.

The study was guided by a plan of observation—the "Schema." The Schema is set out in the Appendix. My students and I developed the Schema over many years of school observation and interviewing. Its contents are not based on the direct recommendation of principals of excellent schools. Such educators usually do not think of their work in a consciously systematic fashion, or describe their principles in writing—just as Napoleon, the Duke of Wellington,

1

or George Washington never conducted or wrote any deliberate studies on how to fight wars. Putting it simply, it takes different skills to be an able doer, compared to being an able observer or writer.

Still, from extended research, I believe the Schema represents the intellectual framework such educators unconsciously apply in their elaborate but tacit analyses. The Schema, and its rationale, will be readily understood by all persons who complete the book. The Schema can be productively applied to any school in a summary fashion—e.g., a one-hour visit—or through an exhaustive study. In either case, it is a valuable tool to both educators—who wish to assess and improve their own schools or classrooms—or laypersons who want to develop more informed opinions about education. Lay opinions about schools are certainly becoming more important, as parents make more deliberate family choices among different public (or private) schools or residential communities (built around schools), and as other citizens, in roles such as school board members and PTA activists, seek to improve school policies.

One way of characterizing our era is to say that we suffer from a shortage of love objects, i.e., institutions that seem to deserve our vital trust. To my mind, Reilly—and the dedication it signifies—is a deserving love object. It reminds us of the importance of trustworthy local institutions in our lives. For most of us, it is far less significant who governs in Washington, or in the state house, than it is to feel we are well served by our immediate public agencies, businesses, and sites of employment. It is good to know that some Americans still receive such precious support from schools like Reilly.

The rationale for Reilly's selection as my subject is simple. It was identified as an excellent school in a Chicago areawide open competition, which was conducted by the For Character School Award Program, sponsored by the College of Education of the University of Illinois at Chicago. That program was designed and monitored by a broadly representative group of Chicago area educators, plus a few academics. The program has gone through three cycles during the 1980s, each of which has been announced to the approximately 2,000 Chicago area public and private schools. Over the three cycles, a total of about 500 schools requested application forms, and about 300 completed forms were submitted. After deliberate screening, further information was requested from certain designated submitters. There was another screening, and the surviving competitors were then site-visited by teams of educators. Finally, the program's Awards Committee designated a total of fifty-four winners, one of which was Reilly. The Schema essentially covers the criteria applied in the award process. When I planned a one-year study of a school, I chose Reilly from these winners because it was physically convenient, it was

an elementary school (not a high school or junior high), and it was a public school in a relatively difficult environment.

Several years have elapsed between the initiation of my study and the publication of this book. During that period, the individual schools in the Chicago system were placed under the supervision of local school councils. This shift was the result of much publicized state legislation. Readers may wonder if the shift has any effect on the relevance of this study. The short answer is, very little.

I have kept in touch with Reilly since the study, and have a feel for its current situation. The relationship between the school and its parents at the time of my study was excellent—as readers will see. Those relationships, now extended to encompass the school's local council, are still fine. They are fine due to the school's continuing open door policies, its able professional leadership and normal disposition of parents to cooperate with competent people who are trying to help their children. Essentially, the community goodwill the school deservedly enjoyed has continued after the shift from one institutional structure to another. The reform law has done little to change the conclusions presented at the end of the book. Where particular Chicago schools are well managed, council-school relations are often fine and constructive; where schools are poorly managed, it is often hard for a semi-external body, frequently lacking in managerial perspectives, to wisely determine how to interject itself. This is a reason the book focuses on the specifics of excellent day-to-day school management. Such a focus must be an important component of school improvement. Indeed, one aim of this book is to provide laypersons with a lucid explanation of the problems of day-to-day school operation.

A GREAT SCHOOL

In no sense do I propose that all schools should become exactly like Reilly in order to be excellent. Some differences among good schools are inevitable, and essential. They will be larger or smaller—making for differences in operation—and will enroll younger or older pupils. Some schools may be private, or church-related, and others public. There are also factors of locale and institutional adaptation. For instance, the Reilly building was comparatively crowded; this affected the shape of some of its policies. But despite such necessary elements of difference, by the end of this book, readers should be able to identify the spirit that permeates the school, and the policies that reflect and shape that spirit. Many of those policies, and the essence of that spirit, are transferrable and even now flourish in a variety of existing schools.

A few statistics should be recited for background. Reilly has 750 pupils. It covers grades pre-K through eighth. Fifty percent of its pupils are white—many of them of Polish origin. Thirty-eight percent are Hispanic. Seven percent are black, and three percent Asian. About one-third of its pupils were born outside the continental United States. Fifty-seven percent of its pupils come from families federally classified as low income, and entitled to free or reduced-price school lunch (on the average, about thirty percent of all pupils throughout America receive such aid). The school has forty-one staff members designated as teachers, eight clerks, aides and bus attendants, plus maintenance and food service personnel. The faculty is about 75/25 white/black. Twenty percent of the school's pupils travel to Reilly by school busses, to attend various special programs. The building is seventy-four years old, and basically in sound shape, but rather crowded. Mrs. Rosemary Culverwell has been its principal (and acting principal) for fifteen years. During the school year of my visit, it was announced that its previous year's eighth grade reading and vocabulary test scores were 8.7 and 8.5 respectively, and its math score was 8.7. Now, let us see how the year began. . . .

Chapter Two

THE BEGINNING

Stay in School

A lot of kids will tell you,
Don't go to school.
If you do go, Man,
They're going to call you a fool.
Well, I'm telling you now
Go to school and do your work.
Don't drop out,
Or you'll become a jerk.
Listen to your teacher.
Come on, open up your ears.
Work your way through college,
And you'll get a great career.

(Sixth-grade pupil's poem in Sparkles, *the school literary magazine.)*

FEW important events have clear-cut beginnings. The complex debates surrounding abortion, and the question of when human life commences, simply remind us that semi-arbitrary elements underlie the boundaries of most beginnings. And so, for the Reilly school, we can say that the beginning of the school year started with a postponement, which had diverse ramifications throughout the year.

THE STRIKE

Reilly, like other schools in the Chicago system, was scheduled to open on September 9. During the summer, there were intermittent negotiations between the Chicago Teachers' Union and the Board of Education about the board/union contract for the next school year. Everyone knew the negotiations might not be immediately fruitful; during eight of the previous seventeen years, there had been strikes that delayed school openings. As the date of opening neared, it seemed another strike—largely focused on increasing teachers' wages—was likely. On September 4, four days before the first workday, the union held a strike vote of its 24,000 members. Almost all of the members voting followed their leaders' recommendations, and opted for a strike—by a vote of 4,437 to 438. It was interesting that only about 20 percent of the members chose to vote. The low vote reflected teacher ambivalence.

Due to the budget pinch confronting the board and the city, one might be pessimistic about the chances for teachers to obtain a significant increase. On the other hand, the teachers believed they "deserved" a raise, and felt that they had little choice but to back the union. The large proportion of nonvoting teachers meant that most teachers knew a strike was coming; they could not really resist it. However, they did not greet it with enthusiasm. The strike lasted nineteen calendar days (see photo 1). Eventually, the board came up with an offer that the frustrated teachers, and their leaders, deemed acceptable. The union's representative body then voted 563–95 to accept the offer and return to work—subject to the total membership approving of the settlement in a full-membership ballot. And so Reilly school began on Monday, October 5. Students would return to school on the sixth. The restless teachers, children, and parents looked to the revival of normalcy.

THE MEETING

In the Chicago school system, "institute day" means a day on which teachers report for work, but no pupils are present. The time is used for staff meetings and other forms of planning and cooperation. The system designated October 5 an institute day. All of the teachers reporting to Reilly had been assigned there last year, and many of them had been there for several years. They began arriving about one-half hour before the scheduled 8:30 meeting. Many had not been in contact with each other since the end of the last school year—three months ago. Oftentimes, the reunions were

5

spontaneous and warm (see photo 2). Such warmth was consistent with my later perception of the sense of caring that pervaded the school.

The "institute" began in the school library, the regular site for schoolwide teacher meetings. The gathering included all the full-time professional staff assigned to the school. Before the meeting, each teacher received in his/her mail box a variety of documents pertinent to the new year, including a schedule of institute day activities. Mrs. Rosemary Culverwell, the principal, had determined to make the meeting comparatively brief. The teachers had many immediate responsibilities to meet, so classes would be ready to start the next day. Mrs. Culverwell also had other duties to handle in the school. Preparations for the next day were further complicated since the building had been closed during the strike—the service staff was out with the teachers. Thus, it was difficult for school preparations to occur until the strike was settled. Mrs. Culverwell opened the meeting (see photo 3).

She first remarked, "I am happy to say that all of the teachers working with the school at the end of last year will be with us again." This statement triggered spontaneous applause. Mrs. Culverwell made other brief remarks about events affecting staff members—one had a baby, one was absent since her husband had been in a serious car accident (someone asked, "What hospital is he in?"). She then turned to the business of the meeting. At the meeting, teachers were supplied with copies of an elaborate "school action plan."

1

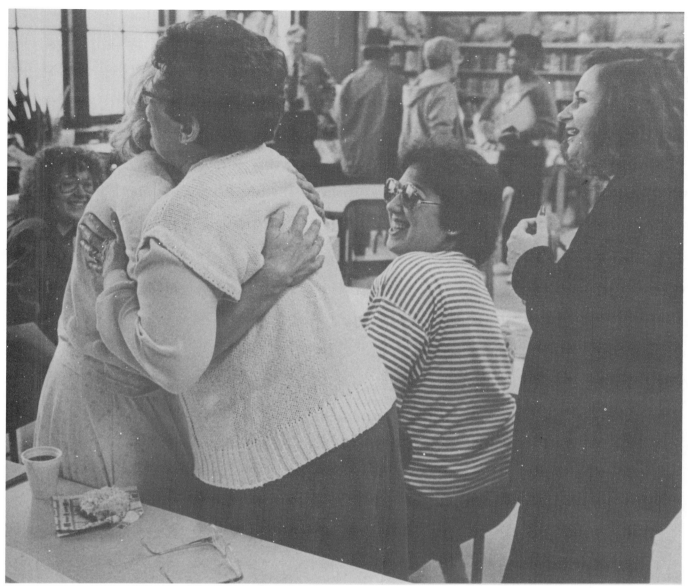

2

The plan was developed over the summer (but before the strike) by Mrs. Culverwell and a faculty committee. The plan followed a format provided by the board. She told teachers that they would be expected to read the action plan, and make check marks in their copy around those portions pertinent to their responsibilities. She said, "In the future, I may collect copies of your lesson plan books, to see how closely you're following the action plan, and coordinating your efforts with the rest of the school."

Mrs. Culverwell made a few other brief remarks, including a reminder about the school's policy that each teacher should strive to recruit at least one parent volunteer to help the teacher and class in appropriate ways. She then announced, in a clear but low-key way, the two alternative

3

sign-out times each teacher had for the day. The alternatives depended on whether teachers chose to take time out for lunch, or preferred simply to work through lunch. That announcement recognized that, on regular school days, teachers had no options about lunchtime—they had to stay with their classes during lunch. But, since they had a choice today, Mrs. Culverwell wanted their sign-outs to reflect that choice on the record. The meeting then adjourned. It had run about an hour. Formally, the teachers might have chosen to raise additional questions, but most of them were anxious to get to organizing their rooms. The meeting disclosed important themes pervading life at Reilly.

There was a sense of community and solicitude; the pleasures of reunion and supportive concerns about the health and welfare of community members. There was also a commitment to planning and coordination, and a polite but clear reminder that staff members would meet certain defined responsibilities. There was no doubt that Mrs. Culverwell had expectations, and assumed they would be met. Within half an hour of the close of the meeting, another example of those themes came to light.

Over the summer, Mrs. Culverwell had obtained from the board a promise to deliver a number of new laboratory tables to the school in the fall. They would be set in the seventh and eighth grade science classroom on the third (top) floor. She had asked Mrs. Patricia Canepa, a teacher who had been designated the coordinator of the seventh and eighth grader teachers, to handle any class moving arrangements generated by the anticipated arrival of the tables later in the fall. (Usually, in this book, people will be designated by their honorific titles, e.g., Mrs., Mr. Such forms of address were routine in the school.) Mrs. Canepa met with Miss Nicks, the upper grade science teacher, to settle the matter. She gradually realized that the matter had larger ramifications. And so, accepting the responsibilities implicit in Mrs. Culverwell's request, she set about confronting the problem.

The current science classroom could not comfortably contain the new tables when they arrived. Thus, it would become necessary to move Miss Nicks to a more appropriate classroom—and to move the other teacher to the vacated room. It then became evident that it would not be best to simply have only the two teachers trade rooms. The vacated science room would not necessarily be the best class site for the dispossessed teacher. Mrs. Canepa enlarged the circle of discussants meeting in the classroom in question. Considerations of student movement on school days also were involved. Students on the third floor moved into science at different periods throughout the day. It was desirable to either cut down the distance of the students' moves, or insure the students were closely monitored during transit to

prevent disorder. The assistant principal, Miss Jayne Swiatek, was added to the discussion. Other teachers were also invited in. The exchanges were relatively good humored, but essentially vexing.

The teachers wanted to get on to decorating and organizing their assigned rooms. However, they could not get started until the issue was settled. One or two teachers had even managed to come into the school early, and were partly through with their decorations, but might now have to tear them down and reassemble them in other rooms. Eventually the whole group, by now about eight persons, went to Mrs. Culverwell's office to settle the matter. Mrs. Culverwell heard all sides, and articulated the frustrating options. She reminded everyone that "when these new tables arrive, the science classes will become more rewarding for students. What's upsetting us now is basically a side effect of a good thing." It was evident Mrs. Culverwell did not want to simply tell her staff what to do about this matter. She was more concerned with developing a consensus around some answer the group identified. I gradually discovered that Mrs. Culverwell often turned over many day-to-day decisions to her teachers. But she also kept in touch with what was decided. She practiced a subtle mix of delegation and personal engagement. Eventually, the group opted for making the move immediately—the next day, rather than waiting until the tables arrived. The necessary classroom changes required all third-floor teachers to move their rooms.

Mrs. Culverwell remarked that she would have to call in the building engineer, Ralph, to arrange for his staff to assist; some of the cabinets and desks were too heavy for the pupils or teachers to move. The group sighed with uncertainty. They expected a certain level of resistance, since Ralph's staff would have other predictable responsibilities during the first days of school. Ralph joined the meeting and engaged in the expected, but relatively good-natured, grumbling. Eventually, he said he could arrange to help and the group left, to make final preparations for the move. Classes began the next day.

Throughout that day, I especially observed five separate teachers who I will follow closely throughout the whole year: Mrs. Helen Estes, in first grade; Mrs. Gloria Windham, in fourth grade; Mrs. Elizabeth Lucas, a teacher of special education pupils between eight and ten years of age; Ms. Bernice Humphery, in fifth grade; and Mrs. Patricia Canepa, a seventh and eighth grade language arts teacher.

MRS. HELEN ESTES

Mrs. Estes has taught at Reilly for about fifteen years (see photo 4). Many Reilly teachers have had similar long service in the school; it was seen as a good place to work, and most teachers wanted to stay there. Her class will be a mixture of first and second year pupils—assigned largely on the basis of reading ability. When I asked her aims for the year, she remarked, "I hope to move the class, on the average, to improve their reading test scores a year and a half." She also observed that "many of my pupils have never been in school for a whole day. Their previous class was a half day kindergarten; and so I hope to help them comfortably adjust to the whole school day. But some elements of trauma will be involved, especially at first."

I entered into Mrs. Estes' class at 9:15, shortly after she had led her pupils in. She talked in a loud, firm, and warm voice. She often referred to herself in the third person. "You know Mrs. Estes knows some of you, but there are other new pupils in this class." She frequently made intergroup comparisons to make her point: "Jimmy and Charles, are you going to act so the new first graders know how smart you are?" She was open to suggestions from pupils, but kept things to the point. One pupil asked, "Were you on strike, too?" She replied, "Yes, I was, everyone was. . . ."

Mrs. Estes had carefully planned her day. She had prepared large name cards for each assigned pupil. She handed them out to the pupils, whom she called individually to her desk. The pupils were told to place the cards at designated spots on their desks. She interspersed formal activities with friendly and cautioning remarks: "Yvonne, your hair's so pretty," or "Charles, are you setting a good example?" She emphasized establishing structure, getting things right the first day.

"Children, when I ask you to stand up at your desks, do it quickly and quietly. You see the gerbil in the back in the cage? Marie, please point out the gerbil to them. He is seminocturnal. That means he sleeps a lot in the day. I want you to get up so quietly that you don't wake up the gerbil. Let's try it again."

Pupils were assigned various tasks, and given titles—separate front and back captains for both the boys' and girls' lines (when groups of pupils moved through the school they kept in line), and two board monitors—who push up the blackboard, set on a slide, so children can use the cloak area. While such patterns of giving pupils "jobs" is common in schools, I found Reilly teachers gave extraordinary emphasis to this policy. Mrs. Estes mentioned, "Each one of you will take a turn in these important jobs." She was intermittently interrupted by school staff members and parents, who came to the door, bringing new pupils in from registration (see photo 5). (Actually, the adult shown bringing in the pupil is Mrs. Kane, the PTA president, who volunteered to help the school on this extra-busy day.) Some of the pupils will stay in the class, while for others it will simply be a

4

5

holding unit, before permanent assignments. For some of the new pupils, it is their first day ever in school. The uncertainty of the pupils, and the affection and concern of their parents, is evident.

Mrs. Estes tried to put the newcomers at ease, reply to the parents' questions, and keep one eye on her class. She managed these tasks quite effectively. Many pupils in the class are foreign-born—either Mexican or Puerto Rican. Some could not speak English. Some parents bringing in new children were also not fluent in English. (Later I will discuss the school's policies regarding foreign-speaking students.) Mrs. Estes adapted to these challenges. One measure she applied was to pair such pupils with other pupils who were bilingual in the appropriate language. By 10:40, Mrs.

Estes had dealt with four new pupils or transfers; handed out name cards; assigned pupils to their seats at tables one, two, or three; collected lunch money; delegated particular responsibilities to some pupils; and explained to them and had them do the Pledge of Allegiance and sing "America, the Beautiful" (she played the piano).

She then had the boys and girls form separate lines to go to the washroom under her supervision. The pupils were provided with paper towels to take with them. (This was in contrast to leaving a roll of such towels in the washroom, and letting the students take as much as they want.) A towel monitor was appointed for each line. Each monitor was told, "Give one full section of towel to every second child. Each student with a towel section will tear it in half, and hand a half to the student behind him. This will help save toweling." I left as the pupils were going out in lines to the washroom.

MRS. GLORIA WINDHAM

Mrs. Windham was one of the newer teachers (see photo 6). Last year she had regularly worked at Reilly as a substitute. Mrs. Culverwell was pleased with her performance, and arranged for her to continue in the school this year teaching an assigned fourth grade class. Mrs. Culverwell often used the substitute system to screen potential permanent teachers. Mrs. Windham was still formally a substitute, since she had not yet completed all the requirements for certification.

Before beginning as a public school teacher, she had taught for two years at a small elementary school in Chicago sponsored by a black Protestant church. Mrs. Windham told me that her largest objective for the next year was to move her students further towards overall competency, according to the curriculum guidelines provided by the school. Unlike the more experienced Reilly teachers I dealt with, she did

not explicitly refer to test score improvement. Mrs. Windham was leading her class through an exercise in sentence construction. The students had textbooks open in front of them. Mrs. Windham was walking throughout the class, calling students semi-randomly to respond to the questions posed in the exercise in front of them. "Semi-randomly" meant that sometimes she called on students who raised their hands, and other times she called on students who were sitting quietly at their desks. As the lesson proceeded, she occasionally had to take measures to emphasize pupil discipline.

In one instance, she directed one of the boys whom she saw as unruly to take a seat on the other side of the room, between two girls. While she was walking around, she pointed to the clock, and emphasized that the lesson would be over at a particular time—in about one-half hour. Students kept writing, and trying to determine what collections of words in their textbooks were complete sentences. By this time, Mrs. Windham had stopped asking for oral recitals. She simply walked around and helped students who raised their hands and asked for it, and occasionally she overlooked some child and intervened to be of assistance. She directed another boy whom she saw as unruly to leave his seat, and sit at her desk. Evidently, she wanted him to be

6

temporarily isolated from other pupils. Sometimes I could detect the act of misconduct that generated her reprimands. But sometimes the triggering instances were lost on me. However, it seemed she had a vision of the decorum she was trying to transmit.

As in Mrs. Estes' class—but less frequently—new pupils occasionally came in. During the next day, I asked her about one new pupil (who had arrived yesterday). She was able to give me a clear statement of why she had assigned this girl to a specific seat, and some general estimate of her ability from overlooking her seatwork—she had not yet received the pupil's test scores from last year. Eventually, the exercise ended. Then, it was lunch. Pupils ate at their desks, since Reilly (like many Chicago public schools) maintained a "closed campus." No pupils went home for lunch; they either bought lunch at school, or brought it from home. While eating, they were supervised by their classroom teachers, who ate with them—and who consequently did not have a significant break during the workday. This policy kept children from being exploited or causing mischief on the streets during lunchtime. In addition, many parents were not home during lunch, so it provided such potential "drifting" children with adult supervision.

The school, like many in Chicago, was not designed to provide eating space for children; its original premise was that children would go home to lunch. Thus, when the children ate in school, they had to eat in their classrooms, supervised by their teachers. The policy shortened the school day for both children and teachers (in-school lunch was half an hour; away-from-school lunch was one hour), although it left teachers more prone to isolation and tension because they had to go through the day without substantial breaks. At Reilly, Mrs. Culverwell consulted each year with the school PTA to see if they supported the closed campus policy, and the group routinely reported that parents preferred it.

Mrs. Windham gave her students significant responsibilities for organizing lunch. Three of them were designated as lunch monitors. They left the classroom before lunch, picked up the packaged lunches and brought them to class. They helped distribute the lunches, and finally assisted in wiping the desks—though the students ate with comparative cleanliness. While lunch monitors were on pick-up, and class continued, a kindergarten teacher came to the door, and spoke briefly with Mrs. Windham. She went over to some seated pupils and recruited two girls. As she left, she emphasized to them, as they remained at their desks, to "remember to have your parents sign the permission slips." I was later told she had recruited these girls to routinely help kindergarteners get dressed for recess on colder days and otherwise assist her in the future. The girls would be regularly excused by Mrs. Windham to provide such help.

THE RECESS

During the morning the first regular recesses occurred, and had become complicated. There were two separate recesses, one for the younger and the other for the older grades; each lasted fifteen minutes. As we will see, recess played a significant part in daily school activities.

Teachers were allowed to take brief breaks during recesses, except for one or two assigned playground duty (the play area had no equipment, and is merely a large asphalt yard). But in the first recess of the first day, most teachers personally supervised their pupils. Mrs. Estes, in particular, closely monitored her relative newcomers (see photo 7). Mrs. Culverwell came out and observed and was distressed. There was too much disorder among the children. She identified the problem: pupils from different classes were not being kept in their assigned areas. She determined to immediately correct things. After the recess, when the pupils were back in class, she made an announcement over the public address system.

All lower grade teachers were directed to again bring out their pupils to the playground at eleven o'clock—a time she estimated would be relatively convenient. When the classes were outside again, she allocated each individual class its specific play area in the yard (see photo 8). Furthermore,

8

9

she clarified the assignments to the pupils who assisted the teachers as playground monitors. When she was completed, each class and its teacher and monitors knew their specified play area. The pupils then returned to their classrooms. Mrs. Culverwell remarked to me that the intervention was a little disruptive. However, it was important that basic principles, such as playground allocation, be quickly clarified. Otherwise, substantial disorder could be generated among several hundred pupils engaged in semi-free play.

Throughout the day, many strange adults were about the schoolyard, auditorium, and office. They were parents bringing new pupils and transfers to be enrolled. A system had been set up in the auditorium to handle such newcomers. But, oftentimes, special situations required visitors to come to the school office. The matter was further complicated since many "special" students also needed deliberate handling—the families might only speak Spanish or Polish, or their children might have special handicaps. Appropriate staff had to handle such contingencies. As much as possible, the school tried to routinize the process. But special situations still arose, requiring the intervention of Mrs. Culverwell, or Miss Swiatek, the assistant principal. All new parents received materials enthusiastically explaining about Reilly, its policies and programs, and inviting them to pro-

vide the school with volunteer help and join its PTA. There were equivalent materials in Spanish and Polish. I believe the tone and clarity of these documents were superior to those typically available at other schools. Throughout the day, as students were registered, they were sent to their classes in session. Oftentimes, their parents went along, to briefly meet the teacher.

MS. BERNICE HUMPHERY, MRS. PATRICIA CANEPA, AND MRS. ELIZABETH LUCAS

After lunch, I visited the classes of Ms. Bernice Humphery, and Mrs. Canepa (whom we first met chairing the upper grade committee). Their learning aspirations for their pupils can be temporarily left in abeyance; their first day was largely dedicated to the moving operation. Pupils were busily shifting desks, books, and other materials through the halls and classrooms on the third floor, (see photo 9), and the heavier furniture was being handled by custodial workers. The moving continued throughout the day. The pupils—understandably—saw it as an interesting lark. The teachers were more frustrated, but essentially good-humored, or at least philosophic. I reflected that the careful deliberation on this issue yesterday left all of the adults convinced that the immediate confusion was a necessary and wholesome solution.

Later in the afternoon, I visited the classroom of Mrs. Elizabeth Lucas. She teaches a small (seven to twelve pupils) class of special education pupils of about ten years of age. Technically they are called Educable Mentally Handicapped, and such pupils are affected with significant mental disabilities. Reilly has been assigned several special education classes. All of Mrs. Lucas' pupils are Hispanic, and oftentimes their English is poor or nil. Language is one criteria for their assignment to this class, since Mrs. Lucas is provided with a Spanish-speaking aide, Mrs. Ingrid Barreto. (Mrs. Lucas' Spanish is limited.) Because of the severity of the pupils' handicaps, most of their schoolwork is handled in this particular class—they are not substantially "mainstreamed." Most of her pupils will be significantly restricted throughout their lives. I had previously briefly interviewed Mrs. Lucas about her aims for the year. She emphasized her pupils' limitations—they learn slowly, and needed a lot of repetition of material. Her goals were to move them towards general efficacy, including matters such as deportment, patience, and moderate skills in literacy and arithmetic.

In adult life, many of her pupils might be able to be self-supporting, and live alone, or in some semi-sheltered situation. (Mrs. Lucas had received training in special education, and taught elsewhere for about ten years before coming to Reilly.) By 12:35, Mrs. Lucas had gotten into the basics of her class. She was taking her students through the exercise of filling in the numbers—1 to 30—on a blank ditto sheet calendar (in the form of a pumpkin face) for October. Later, she mentioned to me that several of the students had "learned" those numbers last year. "But they need a lot of review," she added.

It took a half hour before all of the students completed the thirty figures on the ditto sheet. Getting them through involved breaking down the calendar into five parts—the five Saturdays of the month. As each student completed a week, she examined their work, hugged and patted the pupils, and lauded them with effusive praise (see photo 10). "Mucho bueno, Carlos." "You've really improved, Maria! Mucho trabado." Sometimes, since Mrs. Baretto was working as a translator during registration, she recruited another of her pupils to serve as a translator for another (less English-skilled) pupil. As the pupils moved towards the last day of October on their ditto, she mentioned that Halloween is in October. The school emphasizes that holiday. With the help of her pupil-translators, she explained some of the symbol-

10

ism of Halloween. She focused on the idea of a "witch"—a "brouha." As the pupils finished their numbers, she said, "You have to put your names on such marvelous calendars." And then they were told to hang their calendars on the class bulletin board. I left the school after observing Mrs. Lucas' committed—and successful—efforts at calendar teaching.

THE IN-SERVICE

The next morning began with a half hour faculty meeting in the library. The assembling faculty was more businesslike than before the institute day meeting; reunions had already occurred. Mrs. Culverwell presided. The elaborate agenda consisted largely of announcements (about new and old school procedures) and explanations by Mrs. Culverwell. Some praise was uttered about the successful completion of yesterday's top floor move. Mention was also made of expected new textbooks; the pending revisions of the math program; plans for future half-day in-service sessions; enrollment trends affecting the school; arrangements for pupils using the school library during their assigned time; information that teachers were responsible for having in their grade record books; how to get classroom shades fixed or replaced; how to get chalkboards refinished; and a

reminder not to use pupils as messengers to the teachers' lounge (so the teachers' privacy is respected). The teachers spent most of their time taking notes, though a few questions were asked when teachers raised their hands and waited to be recognized.

Mrs. Culverwell's presentation was informed and cogent. It was evident she expected sympathetic cooperation with her requests. Promptly at nine, the meeting concluded, and the teachers went off to greet and begin their classes. In Mrs. Estes' class, some things were still getting settled. She received at least one new enrollee during the day. This pupil's basic language was Spanish. She had almost no English competency. Mrs. Estes is assigned Spanish-speaking and English-speaking pupils, and the other first grade receives Polish-speaking and English-speaking pupils. Foreign-speaking first graders always attended English-speaking classes. During part of the day, these pupils also went to either Spanish or Polish instruction away from their regular class. At the end of the first grade, these pupils either continued in the English-speaking classes, or were transferred to the full-time bilingual program. Due to this policy, first grade classes contained high proportions of foreign-speaking pupils. I then visited Ms. Humphery's fifth grade class. The class is largely self-contained: the pupils are continu-

11

ously under her direction throughout the day. (This policy will be revised somewhat later in the year.) When asked about her class goals for the year, she mentioned several:

- to have her class attain the best attendance record in the school; two of her classes had done this previously, and she also had twice been the teacher with the year's best personal attendance record
- to have her class advance a year and a half in reading scores
- to have her class learn how to work independently; to begin and carry out their scheduled in-class work without direction and, if a substitute teacher was in charge, to act as if Ms. Humphery was present

Her roll call was being completed. And most of the disorder of yesterday had been corrected, though there were still piles of books and papers in corners of the classroom. She put great stress on pupil discipline. While she was collecting lunch money, a pupil raised his hand and did not quickly catch her eye. The pupil abruptly spoke up about his concern. Ms. Humphery noted the intrusion, looked at the pupil, and shouted, "I didn't ask for that!" He was seated about three feet from her. Her tone and volume even made me jump in my seat. When I later talked to Ms. Humphery about the incident, she stressed she was applying "voice control." She felt this was different from semi-random shouting. Shortly afterwards, she remarked to the class, "If you want to know something, ask the teacher. She is wearing a red top, a blue skirt, and is in front of the room." As Ms. Humphery continued collecting the money, other pupils quietly raised their hands about their seatwork, and waited to get her attention. She sent two pupils away with the lunch money to deliver.

She then began a lesson on yesterday's assigned homework. She had students place their homework on their desks. She observed that, "I want you to shift quietly from one task to another." And the pupils did that. The assignment was on systems of enumeration—tens, hundreds, thousands, and so on. Ms. Humphery had already written on the chalkboard several six or more digit numbers, broken down by columns, into their different values. The writing duplicated the material in the homework. She walked around the class, asking students whom she identified to speak out and provide the correct answers to last night's assignment. As the answers were recited, the pupils graded their work. About half the students she called had their hands raised, and the other half she randomly called by name. Many of the students enthusiastically waved their hands for recognition. Ms. Humphery occasionally sent students to the board, to show how they arrived at their conclusions. Recess time arrived at 10:20, and the pupils left for fifteen minutes in the playground. Ms. Humphery dismissed

12

the rows of pupils with the most orderly—as she designated them—getting up first (see photo 11). She remarked that she was not assigning line captains to the recess; she expected that they could act properly going to and from the school yard.

After recess, I went to Mrs. Canepa's room. She teaches language arts—reading, writing, and literature—to seventh and eighth graders. Her classes are departmentalized: she presents her subject to four separate classes throughout each day. Mrs. Canepa is also assigned a "homeroom," a seventh grade class where she is responsible for guidance and administrative matters concerning her pupils. When asked about her priorities, she did not refer to reading or math scores, probably because her pupils were divided among several teachers. Mrs. Canepa said her goals were to move the classes through spelling; public speaking; composition; learning parts of speech, sentences, and proper usage; and doing research and producing written reports. Hopefully, by the end of the year, the students (depending on their grade level) would all display competency in such matters. In Mrs. Canepa's room, relative order had also arrived after the move. She was returning graded written assignments that had been done by the pupils yesterday, during the moving confusion (see photo 12). She mentioned to her class that the quality of the papers was not good, "Many of them are threes. I have finally gotten to an eight." One pupil, completing some seatwork, balled up a piece of scrap paper, to possibly put in his desk. Mrs. Canepa noticed the noise of the crumpling, and remarked, "Charles, we have an Eleventh Commandment here. Thou shalt not crush paper. This crushing business has infected the class. First Mary, then Louis. . . ." I also recalled similar strictures by Ms. Humphery against paper crushing. The school, and the classrooms, are exceptionally clean. I left the school shortly after the end of recess.

THE UNION MEETING

The next morning, Thursday, October 10, began with a meeting of the teachers—between 8:30 and 9:00—in the teachers' lounge. It was for the union members, to discuss the strike settlement. Under the terms of successive contracts, all teachers were required to be union members (or at least pay union dues, even if they preferred not to join). Even Miss Swiatek, really the assistant principal, was a member—though she probably was also one out of choice. Seventeen teachers attended; there were forty members in the school.

Mrs. Sylvia Gibson, a teacher, was the elected union delegate and presided. Mrs. Culverwell arrived at the beginning of the meeting, to announce that Mrs. Vivian Tamez, the school security guard, was being immediately terminated by the board as a money-saving move to help pay the costs generated by the strike settlement. (Such termination decisions by the board had undoubtedly affected employees at a number of schools.) Mrs. Culverwell thought highly of Mrs. Tamez, and she was well-liked throughout the school. Three years ago, she had begun working in the school as an unpaid, part-time parent volunteer clerk. Eventually, Mrs. Culverwell had gotten her hired in a temporary part-time position as a "bus aide," and she continued to do unpaid office work each day after her bus work was done. When the aide position evaporated, Mrs. Culverwell, with lobbying help from the school PTA, had gotten the school assigned a part-time security guard slot. Mrs. Tamez was designated for that position. She also continued her office work. Now, the guard position was being abolished.

Mrs. Culverwell was partly distressed because of her goodwill for Mrs. Tamez and partly because she lost a dedicated, versatile, bilingual employee. Mrs. Culverwell said she would again try and "save" Mrs. Tamez, but she was not optimistic. The teachers were upset by the board's efforts to cut costs by cutting staff, both immediately and later in the

year. Indeed, some less senior Reilly teachers might end up being transferred, to allow more senior people working elsewhere to keep their jobs by bumping down. Such transfers, from a desirable school to a possibly poor situation, were a distressing contingency.

THE PTA MEETING

About ten minutes after the union meeting, I attended a meeting of the board of the local PTA. It was held in a corner of the school auditorium, because the school lacked other convenient meeting space. The meeting was attended by six mothers, Mrs. Culverwell, and (intermittently) Miss Swiatek. Four children between the ages of two and four played around the auditorium during the meeting. All readers know what a PTA is. In Reilly, the local PTA is a vital organization, which is often not the case in urban public schools.

The Reilly PTA holds meetings, elects officers, affects certain school policies and practices, tries to supply the school with help of various sorts, and otherwise acts like a traditional PTA. Mrs. Culverwell is extremely sympathetic to the PTA's engaged role. She gave the meeting an outline of the rumored layoffs. The layoffs would obviously severely disrupt the school's programs. The members were tense and frustrated. The strike had been distressing, and further repercussions seemed likely. In some ways, the parents' meeting was a replay of the previous union meeting, which Mrs. Culverwell and Miss Swiatek had recently left. There was a considerable amount of undirected tension and anger. Eventually, the mothers decided to write to various officials, protesting Mrs. Tamez's discharge and otherwise pleading the interests of the school. They then turned to planning the year's PTA program.

In particular, they planned for a PTA tea and school tour for October 29. Before the meeting's end, Mrs. Culverwell also reported on other matters, including prospective and completed improvements in school policies—new science materials; arrangements for a music teacher; revisions in the pupil testing program; and bringing more computers into the school. She noted that the funds for these improvements had come from last year's budget, and she was uncertain whether future funds would allow her to continue the improvement process. I returned on Friday, October 16, and briefly visited Ms. Humphery's classroom.

Each classroom conducts a daily Pledge of Allegiance to the flag. It was interesting to see how she handled it. As in all Reilly classrooms, the Pledge is announced and then recited over the public address system by a member of the Student Council. Simultaneously, the students and teachers in each class all stand, hands over their hearts and facing the flag, to recite the Pledge. Ms. Humphery after the Pledge, also had her class sing the first verse of the "Star Spangled Banner" a cappella. She emphasized they should sing with vigor and clarity, out of respect for their country and its flag. She herself led them in the song with brio and skill—"On the count of three, go. One. Two. Three!" It was impressive to hear and see the energy in the students' performance (see photo 13). The Reilly teachers believe that the Pledge is a vital device for starting the school day. Right after the Pledge and Anthem, her class gets to work. Undoubtedly, one reason for centrally announcing the Pledge is to provide all Reilly classes with a defined and prompt starting point.

Teachers are under tacit pressure to quickly begin and complete preliminary activities before the Pledge.

THE HISPANIC PARENTS

I attended a meeting being held in the school for Spanish-speaking parents whose children were enrolled in the school's two separate Spanish language programs. Children from about 100 families are enrolled in the programs. About fifteen parents—twelve mothers and two or three fathers—attended. (For an urban school under such circumstances, that was good attendance.) The meeting was directed by

13

Mrs. Valez, a teacher in the program. Two other faculty members were present. Mrs. Culverwell came in when it was half over, and remained until near the end. The meeting was conducted in Spanish. All English remarks were translated by Mrs. Valez, as when Mrs. Culverwell spoke. The meeting was to inform parents about the goals and mechanics of the program; solicit their advice; choose parents to be officers of the parents' group for the program; and recruit parents to serve as volunteers in their children's classes on a part-time basis, perhaps several hours a week. The meeting proceeded in a friendly and efficient manner (see photo 14).

The parents were interested and supportive. Mrs. Valez, after some cajoling, developed a complete slate of officers. There was no competition for the positions; it was more a matter of encouraging individuals to volunteer, with the understanding that group members might speak out if disagreement existed. Mrs. Valez wrote the designees' names on the chalkboard. Mrs. Culverwell spoke briefly, emphasizing the high quality of the school's teachers, expressing their pleasure with parent attendance, and urging parents to participate in the school's volunteer program. She emphasized that parents would work with the Spanish-speaking staff, and the teachers would be grateful for their help. Mrs.

Valez was then able to get four parents to volunteer. Their names, too, were placed on the blackboard, and they were promptly assigned to particular teachers. They were told the teachers would be in touch with them shortly. The meeting ran about one and a half hours. The parents' meeting touches on an important and unique function of the school: to help foreign-born parents enlist in American life, and rear "American" children.

American urban schools have a long and honorable history of fulfilling this role, and Reilly's situation has been replicated often in our past. A variety of elements of the school's program are focused on this task. Some have already been mentioned: the classes specially designed for foreign language–speakers; staff members with bilingual skills; and efforts, such as the Spanish-speaking parents' group, to give immigrants practice in the forms of the electoral process and otherwise engage them in institutional life. At the same time, there was a concurrent dedication to bringing the families and pupils into mainstream society— hence, Ms. Humphery's stress of the "Star Spangled Banner." Such activities both increase solidarity among foreign parents, and lead them into the overall society. As the year proceeds, there will undoubtedly be further ramifications to this process of Americanization.

15

THE INDOOR RECESS

At 10:15, all classes in the school adjourned for Friday indoor recess. This is a significant feature in the school. "Indoor recess" usually means only that the outside weather is bad. Children, under faculty supervision, "recreate" at their desks, via reading or quiet play. But on Fridays, each class's recess is automatically "indoor"—regardless of weather. The classes are monitored at their desks by pairs of eighth grade pupils, and several teachers and aides who act as overall monitors via walking the halls. The bulk of the teachers go to the teachers' lounge, for a fifteen minute social and coffee break, to mark the end of the week.

It is extraordinary for an elementary school to successfully leave pupils under such thin supervision. It says much about the discipline level of the school. But the procedure is consonant with many of the principles affecting the school's operation—giving unusual authority and responsibilities to pupils, and recognizing the importance of maintaining human relations by providing teachers a chance to socialize. The design of the process is significant. In a number of ways, pupils in the school become accustomed to being supervised by older pupils, and look towards the day when they will move up to such prestigious roles. The matter of teacher socialization is also quite important. During a typical workday, teachers have no separate lunch period, but eat with their classes. They have brief breaks during the day, but can only socialize with those who share that free time. A chance to get together, without any formal agenda, is quite unusual. It is a precious benefit, which costs no one any extra money, for working at Reilly. The atmosphere in the lounge was lively and friendly. Coffee and pastries were set out on a table.

As the teachers assembled, Mrs. Culverwell—who did not always join such gatherings—stepped in, along with Mrs. Tamez. She talked about Mrs. Tamez's important services, and how she would be missed. A farewell card, signed by all of the faculty, was handed to her. One of the teachers remarked that Mrs. Tamez had already taken the civil service exam for potential school clerks, and passed the written part. The typing part was the only challenge left—and everyone knew she would pass that. People shook her hand, and said "Thank you and goodbye." Someone then incidentally remarked, "Who'll sign up to bring the coffee next Friday?" Another spoke up to thank someone for supplying the pastry. And I left for other activities.

Later in the day, I visited Mrs. Estes' class. The children were participating in a letter writing exercise—writing "D O G." They have to apply enormous concentration in the process (see photo 15). Her advice is interspersed with encouragement, and asides: to one child, "Complete means finish," or "I know Antonio is finished, he's sitting quietly with his hands folded," or, "Is it singing time, now, Robert? N o o o."

THE ASSEMBLIES

At one o'clock, the school had the first of its two assemblies of the day, and the first assemblies of the year. On this occasion, there were two assemblies to accommodate the different comprehension levels among the pupils. The first was for primary grades, kindergarten through third. It also included Mrs. Lucas' special education class. The second was for the older pupils. To take her students to the assembly, Mrs. Estes had them line up at the classroom door in single file—boy, girl, boy, girl. They walked into the already partly filled assembly hall. Everyone was seated with relative efficiency. The assembly was opened by the eighth grade boy color guards proceeding down the main aisles, bearing three large flags, and with a fourth boy as commander. The flags were the American Flag, the four-starred flag of the city of Chicago, and a Reilly school flag.

When the colors were on stage, the commander had the assembly rise, and led the Flag Salute. Then a teacher played the first verse of "America" on the piano, and the children sang. The assembly had several themes. Mrs. Culverwell spoke to the students about the school's conduct expectations.

"Do your homework. Know how much homework the school expects of you—about thirty minutes a night at third grade, and smaller amounts for young pupils. Be polite to teachers, parents, and other children. Keep the school neat and clean, like your homes. Always be on time; important things happen at the beginning of classes."

She complimented the pupils on their good manners in the assembly. Her remarks were clearly adapted to the age level of her audience. Miss Swiatek then came on stage to make presentations to the individual students and the lower-level class with the best attendance records for last year. (Indeed, one reason for the assembly was to encourage each class to try and win the contest for this year.) Miss Swiatek emphasized the importance the school gave to good attendance. Recognition was to be provided to classes with the best average attendance records, and individual pupils with excellent records. Mrs. Ward's last year first grade class was designated the winner. Mrs. Ward stood up to receive applause, and Miss Swiatek then mentioned the second grade classes in which Mrs. Ward's former pupils were now enrolled. Then about one-third of the pupils in the assembly were called to the stage by name. When all were present, they were awarded pens and certificates to recognize their perfect attendance for the second half of the last school year. (To ease the movement of almost 100 pupils to the stage, Miss Swiatek had earlier developed a list of the classes now attended by each of last year's winners, so they could be called in order from their current classes.)

The color guards returned to the stage, and paraded off the stage up the aisles with their flags. The assembly was then dismissed at 1:30. In a few minutes, the upper grade pupils filed in for their assembly. It largely followed the format of the preceding assembly with remarks by Mrs. Culverwell and Miss Swiatek. But the tone of the remarks was adapted to the students' higher levels of comprehension. One difference was that, immediately after the Flag Salute, the officers and delegates of the Student Council were inducted. They had been elected to their positions at the end of last year. They came only from the upper grades. The four officers were, coincidentally, all girls. Miss Nicks, the teacher who served as council moderator, oversaw the induction on the stage. She administered the promise to the President, "I promise to do my best to help make Reilly a better place to work and learn."

The President then inducted the other three officers. They then called the twenty-one delegates—thirteen boys and eight girls—to the stage, by name and collectively had them recite the pledge. Throughout the assemblies, the pupils were orderly, and relatively interested. Some of the teachers remained seated, while a few, including Ms. Humphery, stood up or patrolled the aisles to deter inattention or disorder. Mrs. Culverwell, when not on the stage, stood on the side, where she could observe the whole scene. The assembly ended at 2:20. As the pupils filed out and back to their classes, the teachers continued to monitor them. When Ms. Humphery was dissatisfied with her class's conduct going up the stairs, she had them stop, and walked between the two lines, distributing appropriate stares and remarks.

The school makes a production of its assemblies. Running them well takes planning and teacher diligence. When several hundred pupils are brought together, small adult mistakes can generate considerable disorder. The principal and the faculty believe assemblies are valuable. They allow the school to articulate and reemphasize its goals—pride, cooperation, and obedience. They enable Mrs. Culverwell to observe the classroom management capabilities of her teachers, since good classroom discipline translates to good assembly discipline. As we will see over the year, assemblies are used to establish a framework for many school priorities.

Chapter Three

INTO NOVEMBER

Teachers' Grade Record Books

Teachers must be able to verify the basis on which they rate pupils' progress. For this reason it is necessary to keep records of tests, homework assignments, book reports, etc. District Five teachers are to use a grade book provided by Reilly School in which a minimum of three grades in each major subject area per week are to be kept. All grade column headings must be identified, e.g., "Homework," "Unit Test," "Recitation." Send these grade record books to the office with your lesson plan book on the first Tuesday of each month.

(One of ten items in the third bulletin—dated October 20—from Mrs. Culverwell to teachers.)

ON Monday, October 19, I attended a meeting of the school's "discipline committee," a teacher committee newly formed this year. This was the first of many meetings of teacher committees I attended. It is a good place to generally explain the important role of staff committees in the school.

COMMITTEES

Reilly committees ordinarily meet between 8:30 and 9:00 on school days. Since the teachers are required to arrive at school by 8:30, the 8:30–9:00 slot is usually available. The school has a large number of committees and equivalent groups—about fifteen—which meet frequently. Their regular meeting times are announced in a beginning-of-the-year bulletin to teachers, and reminders are posted on the school calendar, kept beside the teachers' sign-in sheet in the front office. The meetings are guided by prearranged agendas developed by the committee chair, and result in minutes produced by the teacher designated as secretary. Copies of each

of these documents are circulated to committee members and also to Mrs. Culverwell. Each teacher usually serves on two committees. Almost all committees are chaired by teachers. On the average, teachers have two meetings each week, of either committees or equivalent groups. The committees include Language Arts, Art, Social, Publicity, Attendance, Safety, the three grade level groups, and ad hoc committees, such as Graduation.

The committees serve a variety of purposes. They enable the administration to transmit and explain school procedures to the assembled faculty representatives. They allow the faculty and school staff to send information and proposals up the line. They provide a means of planning and coordinating the activities being done in different parts of the school. Furthermore, the teachers' committee work stimulates them to be concerned with the overall school, and not just their particular classrooms. Almost all schools have committee systems. Who can be against coordination? However, often such committees are relatively dormant, and largely exist for the sake of appearances. Too frequently, either teachers don't want to do, or don't know how to do, the substantial work involved, or principals don't want or don't know how to delegate. In contrast, the Reilly system is especially complex and vital (largely due to the determination of Mrs. Culverwell).

Reilly teachers spend more time in meetings, and spend it more productively, than do most other teachers. We will see many other committee activities throughout the year at Reilly. As we do, we will become more conscious of how the teaching responsibilities of each faculty member are aided by the support from the school's committees.

The discipline committee met in an empty classroom. As a result of a heavy early season snowfall, two teachers assigned to the committee (including Mrs. Talbert, the chair) phoned to say they would be late. By 8:35, six people were present, including Mrs. Culverwell, Miss Swiatek, Mrs. Canepa, and Mrs. Estes. Mrs. Culverwell, who had originally come as an observer, acted as temporary chair.

Mrs. Culverwell began by outlining the goals of the committee—not really administering discipline, but providing counselling, by committee members, to students with ad-

16

justment problems. Such counselling might involve a number of meetings between a student and his/her "counsellor." Technically, each student's teacher plus Miss Swiatek, had such counselling responsibilities. However, Miss Swiatek also had many other duties, and sometimes troubled students might benefit from talking to an adult other than their regular teacher. And so the committee might more accurately be called the counselling committee.

It was mentioned that the teachers serving on the committee would conduct their counselling sessions during the limited free time periods they had during the school day. The principal would, if possible, also find ways to provide extra relief to counsellors, by occasionally assigning free staff members to cover their regular classes. In preparation for the meeting, Miss Swiatek had drafted a set of forms to be used by individual teachers to refer students for counselling (see photo 16). Making the drafts had obviously involved quite a bit of work. The forms asked teachers to clearly identify a pupil's problems, and suggest possible solutions. A well-completed form would simplify the work of each teacher-counsellor. Completing the form might even inspire teachers to invent ways to help their pupils without carrying through a referral.

The discipline committee is a typical example of how school committees can simplify the demands made on teachers. The committee provides a resource for any teacher with an especially recalcitrant pupil. Of course, committees, themselves, have "costs." The work of the committees is done by classroom teachers. But, in most Reilly committees, such teams achieve goals that could not have been attained by individual separate efforts. The drafts pleased the members. They planned to send them out to teachers, and prepare to handle the expected referrals. Mrs. Culverwell remarked that, before confirming such plans, she would contact the two absent committee members, to insure they agreed with this approach. The committee adjourned, and the teachers went to their incoming classes.

Several days later, Mrs. Culverwell told me of the meeting's sequel. Mrs. Talbert arrived shortly after the meeting ended. Unlike the other committee members, she felt the proposed forms were inadequate. She called another committee meeting for the next morning. At that meeting, the forms were reconsidered. Many committee members agreed with her criticisms. It was then decided to revise the forms before sending them out. Mrs. Culverwell regarded the story as an example of a faculty member exercising healthy initiative. Mrs. Culverwell also remarked that oftentimes teachers were too prone to accept proposals put before them, rather than getting engaged in constructive criticism. From my experience as an observer, one cause for such semi-passivity is the tight schedule that teachers must work under. Half-hour meetings just don't allow people much time for exploratory discussion.

IN CLASSES

The next afternoon (Tuesday, October 20), I visited Ms. Humphery. Her students were doing desk work, related to their "work folders." Each student had a personal folder, with a unique and conspicuous cover, designed by the student. The folders were kept in neat piles at the front of the class. The pupils' graded papers and other work products were kept in the folders. The students were examining and working on materials for their folders. Meanwhile, Ms.

Humphery walked around the class, overseeing their work, and providing pupils with private and public praise and criticism (see photo 17). In the front of the class, several students chosen by Ms. Humphery were updating the materials in some of the students' folders. In effect, the students were Ms. Humphery's aides. Students occasionally raised their hands, and quietly waited for Ms. Humphery to come over and consider their questions.

I noticed that Ishmael, a student I saw her sharply rebuke a few days ago, had his hand up for a long time before getting her attention. Later, I discussed this "wait" with her. She confirmed my suspicion that she had especially stretched out his wait, to give him training in patience and persistence. She felt Ishmael was coming along reasonably well.

17

THE STUDENT COUNCIL

Towards the end of the school day, I attended the first meeting of the recently inducted Student Council. The council had about twenty-five members from grades four through eight. Usually, the council met weekly. Student councils are common in schools. But the level of vitality of such councils varies widely—from significant and engaged groups to moribund ones. Understandably, the main factor determining their efficacy is the leadership provided by adults. Part of the problem is the very nomenclature applied to such groups—"councils."

The term "council" implies weighty responsibilities, or even authority. But, especially at the grade school level, councils are best perceived as service clubs—groups of students organized to plan and carry out activities of benefit to the school under general adult supervision. In this process, a council may have some discretion, but it is unrealistic to consider a council part of a school's governing machinery.

Miss Nicks, the council faculty moderator, had a realistic view of the council's potential. Speaking to the whole group, she outlined the responsibilities of the new officers: the president and vice president presided; the secretary took attendance and kept records; and the sergeant at arms placed delegates in appropriate seats. She announced that the council's first assignment was to publicize the forthcoming Science Fair. Council members in the lower grades were asked to take posters (saved from last year) advertising the fair and put them up in their classrooms, and otherwise spread the word about the fair (e.g., by making announcements to their classes). Older pupils would touch up posters from earlier years that needed revision, and make some new ones.

Another Student Council responsibility is providing council members to lead the school's daily Pledge of Allegiance ceremony. Each day, a designated council member goes to the school office and leads the pupils throughout the school in the Pledge. A roster was developed so each council member led such salutes several times a year. Older and more experienced members were designated to oversee and train the younger members. The council officers developed such a roster during the meeting, with some encouragement by Miss Nicks.

The next day I asked Mrs. Windham and Ms. Humphery about their contacts with pupils' families so far this term.

19

Each of them estimated that so far they had about six contacts via notes, phone calls, or visits to school. In the afternoon, on Friday, October 23, I visited Mrs. Windham's class. As her class proceeded, she occasionally noted the names of misbehaving pupils on the chalkboard, and put checks beside those names if the pupils committed more infractions. During the visit, I saw that her "problem boy" had twelve checks; the next highest pupil had five. (It was also interesting that 70–80 percent of the pupils listed were boys.) The boy was assigned a seat in the girls' section of the class. Still, even in apparent isolation, he found ways to enlist allies in his mischief-making (see photo 18). In Mrs. Lucas' room, she was working with the pupils to decorate paper plates, with man-in-the-sky faces. Some of the pupils were pleased to say the faces resembled Killer Robots. Mrs. Lucas cheerfully accepted the new designation.

Finally, I visited Mrs. Estes' class. The last half hour of their week was playtime. It was striking to see the contrast between the play choices of the boys and girls. Most of the girls went over to the chalk board, and began writing and "teaching." The boys generally favored more directly physical activities, involving toy trucks and rockets. A few of the pupils of both sexes worked on completing their painting of large paper bags as pumpkins—part of Halloween preparations (see photo 19).

THE PTA GET-ACQUAINTED TEA

On Thursday, October 29, the PTA held its tea and get-acquainted meeting in the library. Immediately before that gathering, the parents of the children in the Polish program met separately, under the leadership of Ms. Nocula, a teacher in that program. There were about twenty parents at that meeting. It was understood that these parents would come to the PTA tea after concluding their meeting. The PTA meeting was opened by Mrs. Nelson, the program chair. She led the group in the Pledge of Allegiance, and then recited the PTA prayer. Someone in the group mentioned that they had already recited the Pledge earlier in the meeting — before many members of the group had arrived. Mrs. Nelson said it was a good practice to allow everyone to participate in the Pledge, and went ahead as planned.

About thirty parents were present, plus the Polish parents who entered later. From my experience with Chicago schools, I would say that the meeting had good attendance. The PTA officers were introduced, and its role in the school explained. Mrs. Culverwell was introduced, and said a few words. The program chair then introduced an outside speaker, who spoke for thirty to forty minutes. He was Mr. Patrick Bowers, the executive officer of the Save Our Neighborhoods coalition. He spoke on necessary reforms in Chicago public schools. Mr. Bowers distributed literature to the audience, and discussed the thrust of the reforms proposed by his group and its allies. In a distorted way, some of his points were relevant to the Reilly school situation. He said that parents should have a significant role in managing local schools, rather than simply acting as aides and volunteers assisting the professionals. He urged each parents' group to enlist (for free?) the services of experts in tests and measurement, to analyze and criticize their particular school's testing programs. And, in general, he presented a bleak and adversarial view of parent/school relations. The presentation was comparatively irrelevant to Reilly.

Though the school PTA is active, it is not particularly interested in changing significant school policies — though members have their dissatisfactions with the board, the next level of management. The school's test scores compare favorably with those of other schools in the system. The PTA hopes to involve more parents in school activities, and so does Mrs. Culverwell. But Mr. Bowers had no concrete suggestions about how to improve their already active outreach. The issue of parent involvement is a good instance of the ambiguous rhetoric of school reform. Few, if any, authorities are against "parent involvement." But the phrase has many different meanings, ranging from parents being frequently present around school, to having organized groups of parent representatives making substantial and immediate decisions about policy, e.g., how frequently teachers should have committee meetings, or how a principal should be evaluated. Sloganeering is common in education. It prevails because vast numbers of people are affected by schools, as parents and employees. Furthermore, parents are understandably impatient with incrementalism — they naturally want immediate benefits for their children. These forces create powerful tendencies towards oversimplification. But operating schools is inherently a complex activity.

This complexity argues for incremental reform — Gordian knots must be untied, and not cut. Thus, there is a constant tension between the need for incrementalism and deliberation, compared to an electorate affected with urgency. Sometimes the outcome of such tension is either cynicism, or erratic, and ill-conceived reforms. One encouraging element involves the stabilizing forces that often permeate schools. Many current and inherited education policies may be short-sighted and simplistic. However, schools — and the people who work in and around them — are affected by enormous constructive influences. Such influences touch on powerful incentives, like human love, beauty, and joy. Thus, reform should often be more a matter of strengthening the many health-seeking forces in schools, rather than emphasizing new, and relatively oversimplified, remedies.

AN INVITATION

In late October, Mrs. Culverwell received an invitation to attend a reception to be held on the evening of November 17. It was in honor of Mrs. Ada Lopez, a newly designated member of the Chicago Board of Education. The party was sponsored by Mrs. Arcelis Figueroa, the Superintendent of District Five. This district was the Chicago school system's administrative unit, which supervised Reilly. There are twenty-six elementary schools in the district, and twenty districts in the Chicago system. The system's secondary schools were supervised by a separate administrative structure. Mrs. Lopez had recently been designated by the Mayor as a member of the board. It was understandable that the district would throw a party to recognize her attainment. The party was being held in the lobby of a bank serving a neighborhood that was part of the district. I asked Mrs. Culverwell whether it would be appropriate for me to attend. She said, "Certainly." And so I sent in my $15 check. Meanwhile, of course, things kept going on at Reilly.

Before classes began in the morning on Tuesday, November 3, I visited several teachers. In Mrs. Windham's room, I found a mother and her daughter talking with Mrs. Windham. The daughter was one of her pupils. The mother was temporarily unemployed and had volunteered time to help Mrs. Windham. The "help" required a little ingenuity.

20

The mother only spoke Polish. However, Mrs. Windham, using the daughter as a translator, designed an assignment for the mother, grading students' papers. The mother had a correct paper put before her, and simply noted the errors in the papers she graded. On Tuesday, the daughter had come in with her mother before class. She had brought in, to show Mrs. Windham, a thick display book of the awards she had won in competitive swimming—plus some of her trophies. She was delighted to show these materials to Mrs. Windham, and Mrs. Windham was warmly appreciative. The mother, too, was pleased with her daughter's display, and Mrs. Windham's response (see photo 20). I later realized the episode was typical of Reilly's strong open door policy toward parents.

INTRODUCING PHONICS

In Mrs. Estes' room, a transition was occurring. The pupils were about to start their work in phonics. Both first grade teachers, Mrs. Estes and Mrs. Lange, had attended a special class to learn the approach. Mrs. Estes had the students line up by the chalkboard, and each student drew a long chalk line down from the top of the board. The students were then told to write particular letters of the alphabet in their columns with chalk, and were individually called on to read off each letter in a loud, clear voice (see photo 21). Mrs. Estes led the whole exercise with enthusiasm, clarity, and a certain degree of gravity—the activity was important. The children responded appropriately.

21

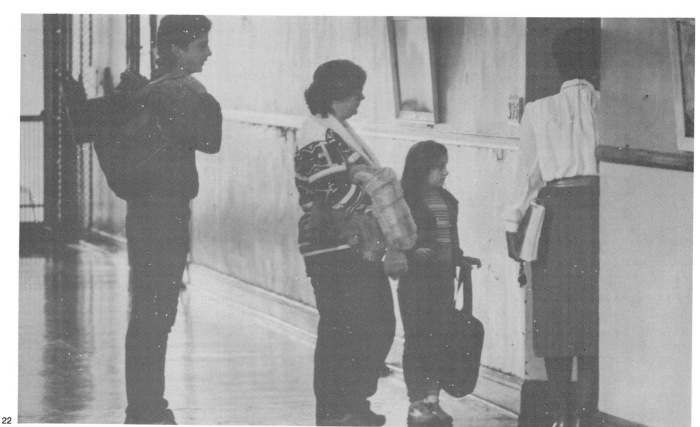

22

The matter of "transitions" touches on another theme that affects classroom life at Reilly, and all other schools. Students have to pass through a number of transitions each school day. In the upper division—grades seven and eight—they shift among several teachers and classrooms each daily. (Remember how the upper division teachers, before students arrived, developed a plan for the science classes, so students would have orderly transitions among classrooms?) Students also collectively leave their classrooms for recess and to go to the washroom. And, even in lower grades, students often shift through different subjects during the day; or, as in Mrs. Estes' beginning of phonics, they shift from one form of instruction to another. Furthermore, even young pupils, in many instances, as in the bilingual program shift among teachers throughout a day.

During such transitions, it is "natural" for students to have their attention drift, as they disengage from present activities, and emotionally and/or physically move elsewhere. Over the school day, a great deal of instruction time can be lost through disordered transitions. As a result, most Reilly teachers, especially during the first few days of the year, drill their classes in making quiet and prompt transitions.

I next visited the school on Tuesday, November 10. I arrived before classes began. As I walked about the third floor, I saw a mother and her two children going from classroom to classroom (see photo 22). The mother was arranging her son's readmission to school. He had been suspended until a parent came to school to discuss his discipline problems. Oftentimes, the school used the suspension process as a tool to provoke parents (who were sometimes reluctant to come to school, despite many calls from teachers) of certain unruly pupils to meet with the child's teachers. Further down the hall, I happened to notice two of the pupil stairway guards doing homework as they waited for the school to open. Such monitoring responsibilities were routinely assigned to eighth grade pupils. The guards entered the building before the official opening time, to be ready to monitor when students were admitted. During my visits, I saw that such students, allowed in the school without close supervision, generally conducted themselves in a responsible fashion. The guards system is part of the Reilly student admittance procedure.

In many schools, teachers come down to the playground, and accompany their pupils to class. In Reilly, the pupils are monitored to their rooms by eighth graders, while teachers wait at their room doors. The procedure saves the teachers' time. As I walked by one classroom, I heard sounds of animated congratulations. Mrs. Drexler and Mrs. Gartner, two of the special ed teachers, were examining a large poster board, containing a number of mounted photographs (see

23

photo 23). Mrs. Drexler had taken the photos of the Reilly special ed students competing in last year's Chicago-area special education Olympics. She had mounted them, and brought them in for Mrs. Gartner to see. Mrs. Gartner was excited and pleased. While her students had participated, she had forgotten the photographs had been taken. She knew her students would also be excited to see the pictures. Later in the week, the display was posted outside the school office on the first floor. When morning classes were in session, I visited Mrs. Windham's room.

I arrived when she was holding at-her-desk conferences with pupils (see photo 24). On such occasions, she would remain at her desk, while pupils worked at seatwork. Pupils would then visit her, either on their own initiative, or by her calling them to her. She would talk over their work progress, or other matters she or the student wanted to pursue. My impression is that the students found this individualized process very satisfying.

RECESS

On several days during this period, I went outside to observe the pupils' recess. During lower grade recess, a number of older pupils also acted as monitors. They helped younger children get dressed in cold weather, prevented significant disorder, and organized and directed games (see photo 25). I particularly saw one monitor, leading a game of

24

jumping jacks on a chilly morning—to keep the younger children active and warm (see photo 26). Several adult aides also were outside overseeing activities. While observing in classrooms, I also noticed that the childrens' gratification at recess gave teachers one convenient, significant, but low-key punishment to apply—denying wrongdoers recess, or making them stay behind to make up incomplete school-work.

From seeing many other schoolyards, it is evident that children's play at Reilly is especially animated and orderly. The tone reminds me of a nineteenth century Winslow Homer painting, *Crack the Whip*, which portrays children playing with their teacher in a country schoolyard. The fact is that children do not "naturally" know games. Games must

be taught. Furthermore, in some games, there must be leaders to monitor or referee disputes. In certain environments, the instruction or leadership occurs via the interaction of younger and older children (or sometimes the direction of adults). In too many schoolyards today, the child-to-child, or adult-to-child relationships that evolve do not foster wholesome play. In particular, the children—especially younger ones—are bounded into their class groups. Then, there are no older children generally motivated to teach the younger ones how to play mildly complex games. And teachers (or the other adults) supervising the children usually only provide them with simple monitoring: no fights. As a result, many pupils merely "hang around," or engage in other, not always desirable activities.

26

27

As children get older, sometimes some of them do or-ganize games, because they have learned how to play in other environments, or their organizing capabilities have increased. Speaking technically, in our era the average age of children beginning to participate in reasonably complex play is probably much older than in the past. However, in Reilly, policies have been deliberately designed to en-courage healthy interaction between pupils of different ages during recess. (I wonder how many Reilly pupils eventually chose to become teachers, partly because of the pleasures they derived from helping younger pupils?)

The play capabilities of Reilly pupils have actually been enriched by the play area's lack of formal structures, e.g., swings, jungle gyms. The open spaces, sometimes with game boundary lines painted on them, really invited more active, cooperative, and imaginative play. But such complex activities require some guidance from older children or adults.

ABOUT RECORDS

On November 12, a half day in-service was scheduled for the school library. It was for all the faculty, plus interested PTA members. An "in-service" is an occasion for the staff to participate in an organized training activity, while the children are kept home from school. Students had the after-noon off, and the teachers attended the session on paid time. The school—or, more properly, a faculty committee—was responsible for planning some of such training sessions, while Mrs. Culverwell was responsible for the others. The session largely consisted of a presentation by Dr. Fred Hess, the Executive Director of the Chicago Panel on Public School Policy and Finance. The panel, under his supervi-sion, had recently conducted a much publicized study of patterns of dropouts in Chicago public schools. He summa-rized the findings of the panel. In passing, he also observed that Reilly had an unusually low level of dropouts among its graduates in Chicago high schools; it was in the ninth per-centile among Chicago public elementary schools in levels of high school dropouts. He congratulated the school with evident enthusiasm for the excellent job of preparation it was doing. His presentation was received with mixed in-terest among the teachers.

Some teachers listened carefully to his obviously in-formed statement (see photo 27). Others, seated at the library tables, busied themselves with the paperwork that often presses on teachers, especially at Reilly—grading papers, entering grades in gradebooks, completing forms, preparing materials to be distributed to students. (I say "especially at Reilly" because Mrs. Culverwell is insistent on teachers giving significant homework, and providing her with timely written reports.) This matter of paperwork will come up again, but might well be considered here.

Teachers rely, to a large extent, on documents to direct and monitor pupil learning. They assign homework, written drills, and tests. These papers must be reviewed by the teachers, and oftentimes pupils should receive back grades or written evaluations. To some degree, the more paper demands teachers generate, the more students will learn. In addition, teachers should keep records of these documents, so they can compute students' quarterly and final grades. Furthermore, teachers are—and should be—accountable to others: pupils' parents, Mrs. Culverwell, and the board in general. Teachers partly satisfy such accountability demands by transmitting written reports—report cards, lesson plans, notes to parents, diverse reports to Mrs. Culverwell, and other agencies of the board. Indeed, we will later see how Mrs. Culverwell relies heavily on such teachers' records to conduct her supervision.

Readers have already probably noticed ways that teachers enlist students and parent volunteers in helping them with paperwork. Furthermore, different levels of paperwork requirements partly depend on the subjects taught, e.g., language arts, compared to physical education. But no doubt some teachers are subject to substantial demands to complete paperwork. Often when I entered a Reilly class, I found the teacher's desk littered with papers in the process of being collected, evaluated, marked up to be sent elsewhere, and so on (see photo 28).

Another effect of the voluminous paperwork is the frequent demand by teachers' unions for smaller classes. The research does not reveal that moderately smaller classes improve pupil learning; however, it is obvious that smaller classes mean less paperwork; fewer pupils means fewer papers to grade. Surely, some of the paperwork demands are unwise, or even mischievous. However, despite such individual flaws, many characteristics of modern schools inevitably generate substantial demands for teacher paperwork. Because of such responsibilities, whenever teachers are asked to attend a meeting for several hours, they subconsciously ask themselves: is it better to sit there and absorb the presentation, or bring along their always lurking papers, and get some more done? Indeed, if teachers sit and attentively listen, one might wonder if they are failing to help their students—by not generating enough paper. True, I rarely saw teachers processing papers at faculty meetings, compared to in-services. Those half-hour meetings were highly work-focused. If the teachers missed some direction uttered at a meeting, they might actually perform their work improperly. But in-services were organized to provide gen-eral intellectual stimulation; teachers felt less obligated to follow every word. Of course, one might also muse about the profitability of particular in-services: did they deserve the attention of most teachers? I cannot directly answer this question here.

One critical point did arise in the in-service discussion. A teacher contended that many Reilly pupils, due to their backgrounds, could not be expected to perform up to national norms. An exchange ensued. Mrs. Culverwell disagreed with this proposition—many Reilly pupils were now attaining or bettering the norms, and she believed that others could be gotten to that point. Dr. Hess invited a show of hands on the issue: could Reilly students, in general, be expected to attain national norms? Of the teachers that voted, eighteen (including Mrs. Culverwell) voted in the affirmative, and eight in the negative. I thought the vote represented healthy optimism. The topic, to my mind, was not one where Mrs. Culverwell's opinion would have a strong coercive effect on the teachers' votes. But it is possible that some of the teachers were simply persuaded by the expression of her respected opinion.

When I left, at the end of Dr. Hess' presentation, I dropped by the office. I noticed Mrs. Barreto, Mrs. Lucas' aide, answering the phone, and otherwise acting as a clerk. This was part of the school's adaptation to Mrs. Tamez's dismissal. Mrs. Culverwell had carried out a variety of staff shifts to cover her leaving. Thus Mrs. Barreto, who was bilingual (like Mrs. Tamez), could occasionally be "borrowed" from Mrs. Lucas, and was placed in the office either during slow times during the school day or from 8:30–9:00, before classes began. I gradually realized that many of the school's employees—aides, counsellors—held responsibilities not suggested by their formal titles. The Table of Organization decreed by the board did not match the school's administrative reality. The principal assumed that she had the discretion to modify the Table in the best interest of the pupils.

THE RECEPTION

Five days later, I attended the reception in honor of the new board member. The bank, the site of the affair, was a couple of miles from the school. It began at five, giving guests time to change, if they chose, before attending— though it was also appropriate to go to work dressed in semi-formal clothes. The only Reilly attendees were Mrs. Culverwell, and Mrs. Rodriguez-Ehrhardt, an uncertified teacher in the Spanish bilingual program. (She used a hyphenated name to indicate her Hispanic background.) I assume Mrs. Rodriguez partly attended to strengthen her ties with the Hispanic community and the Spanish language program.

The photo (see photo 29) transmits some of the spirit of

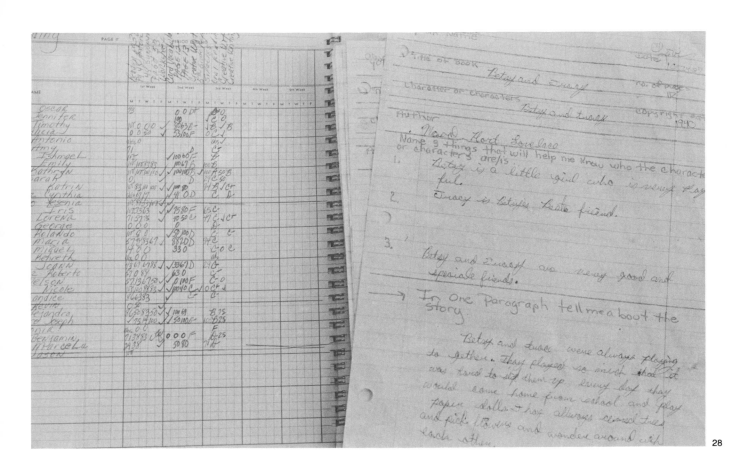

28

29

the occasion. It shows a group on the podium, about to introduce Mrs. Lopez. They include Mrs. Figueroa (the District Superintendent); Ms. Higginbotham, a staff member from the district office; and Mr. Figueroa, Mrs. Figueroa's ex-husband, a local alderman. I was impressed by the good spirits pervading the gathering, and the patterns of ethnic diversity—and homogeneity. "Diversity" because the gathering included many Hispanics, whites, and blacks (and men and women). "Homogeneity" because almost all of the Hispanics, according to an informed guest, were of Puerto Rican background (as are Mrs. Figueroa and Mrs. Lopez). But many Hispanics in Chicago are Mexican-Americans. Even the several visiting Hispanic staff members from the board headquarters were of Puerto Rican background. The music for dancing was also provided by a combo of Puerto Rican performers and a singer. The ethnic politics of the situation—and the board, in particular, and Chicago, in general—are very complex.

Mrs. Figueroa was formerly a candidate for city alderman from the area. The community immediately around the bank is largely Puerto Rican. The overall district is a mixture of Polish and Puerto Rican residents. The Poles are gradually undergoing a political decline—as their urban demographic base diminishes. However, the area's congressman is Polish. He has been in office a long time, and he holds a prestigious position in the House of Representatives. But his eventual successor may be Puerto Rican. Mrs. Figueroa has announced that she is a candidate for the Democratic congressional nomination in the next primary. She may not have a good chance of beating the incumbent, but she will at least uphold the Puerto Rican cause. But we should not assume that, ethnically speaking, the "Puerto Rican cause" is congruent with the overall "Hispanic cause" in Chicago. Indeed, there may even be some tensions between several apparently similar groups: the Mexican-Americans, the Puerto Ricans (who are automatically "Americans"), and other Hispanics, such as Cuban-Americans. Finally, we should recognize that these potential tensions may extend beyond electoral politics. They can even affect who the mayor appoints to the Board of Education, and advancement at certain levels in the board hierarchy.

During many earlier eras of American history, white, upper-middle-class "reformers" aggressively intervened in urban educational politics. One of their aims was to prevent public schools from becoming balkanized ethnic preserves. However, some current political theorists view such tendencies with favor. The goodwill at the party was gratifying. But one might wonder whether the complexities of maintaining inter-ethnic harmony and ethnic solidarity may conflict with the simple goal of rational efficiency.

Chapter Four

GENERATING
FEEDBACK

Dear Colleagues,

The Reilly School Social Committee is the link uniting its members. Each of us wishes to offer congratulations to a colleague on a marriage, or a new baby; to say farewell to one departing; to offer what comfort we can in illness or bereavement. We all enjoy a good party. We hope the Social Committee fulfills these functions for all of us. The Social Fund, which makes this all possible, needs replenishment.

(Solicitation note to all faculty from the Reilly Social Committee).

ON December 9, the teachers will deliver to parents the first report cards. There are four report card deliveries annually. Two of the occasions involve parent in-person pickups in school. In addition, Mrs. Culverwell will soon begin her yearly cycle of teacher evaluation. As such complex activities drew near, many other events were also occurring.

ART IN REILLY

The school actively celebrates Illinois Art Week in the week of November 15. Mrs. Culverwell is a strong proponent of art activities, and is an amateur painter on her own. Indeed, in my own impressionistic research, I have observed that a very high number of able principals possess considerable artistic interests, in music, drama, etc. One principal, when assigned to run a disordered high school, made reorganizing its art department a top priority. Another principal went to great and successful efforts to bring a very able teacher—who specialized in dramatics—to her ghetto grade school. All of these principals also closely monitor pupil test score progress. The principals understand art is an important tool for building bridges among pupils and faculty, and can provide special gratifications to many pupils.

A committee of teachers had been designated to plan Art Week. They collected suggestions and information from teachers and identified relevant activities. Special materials for art projects were also brought into the school. Different classes accepted responsibility for decorating parts of the halls. The pupils and teachers in one preschool class painted an idyllic countryside scene, related to the landing of the Pilgrims (see photo 30). Other classes selected different, but appropriate, themes. The themes portrayed in the art projects nicely demonstrated the school's philosophy about its multi-ethnic population: they display respect for the pupils' diverse cultural traditions, but simultaneously emphasize the overarching theme of their "Americanness."

Apropos of "materials," one incidental matter deserves mention. I doubt that the art materials involved were particularly expensive, but it is relevant for me to recall that in all the time I was in Reilly, I never heard anyone turn down some idea because they did not have the money. I am sure the school could have efficiently spent more money if it had been available, but the feeling was that "crying about lack of money" was unprofessional. It implied that staff members were unable to do their assigned job.

As I watched these activities, I ran across Ms. Humphery. I asked, "Is your class undertaking some special project for Art Week?" She gave a frustrated sigh, and replied, "Don't tell anyone, but we're not, cause I don't have the time." Her reaction emphasized the spirit underlying many Reilly activities: some things were mandatory, others were strongly encouraged (but teachers could occasionally opt out without risking disapproval), and other things were purely optional. I concluded that Art Week was in the strongly encouraged category; furthermore, I sensed that it was generally believed that Ms. Humphery was a "good soldier," and could occasionally be allowed some license.

On the morning of Wednesday, November 10, I visited the school. I wanted to see the opening of the school's participation in the Chicago adopt-a-school program. Under that program, particular area businesses are encouraged to "adopt" a local public school. "Adoption" meant that the business, in ways appropriate to its structure, enters into a supportive and special relationship with its adopted school. They would outline the plan of cooperation for the year. As

30

31

40

I arrived just before classes, I ran across the bank representatives—Ms. Maria Fredone, and Ms. Margaret Surma—entering the building. As the day proceeded, I realized that Ms. Fredone was of Hispanic background, and Ms. Surma had been born in Poland; after her family had emigrated to the United States, she had attended Reilly as a child. Both ladies now held responsible jobs with the bank. I assume that the bank deliberately selected two representatives who might especially reach some current Reilly students.

Shortly after the opening of school, I attended the adopt-a-school assembly. The two representatives had carefully organized their presentation on the program, and the general nature of the bank's operations. Essentially, over the year they planned to inform students—in a variety of ways—of the relationship between their instruction as students and the responsibilities of employees in environments such as the bank. The presentation was fairly lengthy—about an hour altogether. The students were quiet and respectful. It was not clear that many of them were actively interested. After the assembly, Mrs. Canepa mentioned to me that she felt the materials were very relevant. I asked her if she would ask one of her classes to write out short, evaluative notes about the assembly: "Did you think it was good or bad, and why?" She could then turn the notes over to me. The class willingly cooperated.

The notes were relatively negative. Two-thirds to three-quarters of the students disparaged the presentation. The majority of the critics were boys. They felt it was relatively tedious and irrelevant—"After all, I don't expect to work in a bank." I suspect a number of factors underlie this rejection:

(1) Both presenters were female. Their work images did not appeal to young, lower-middle–class males.

(2) A one-hour presentation, composed largely of "lectures," delivered to about 150 pupils, is too formal. It takes considerable experience and insight to design a presentation appropriate to students.

(3) The seventh and eighth grade pupils, especially the males, are a difficult group to reach.

Despite the inauspicious beginning, the highly incremental principles of the communications program seem very sound. If the bank continues its commitment, its employees will become better at communicating with pupils. The basic message they plan to deliver is inherently sound.

IN CLASSROOMS

In the afternoon, I visited Mrs. Canepa's class. A spelling bee was underway (see photos 31 and 32). Pupils who

32

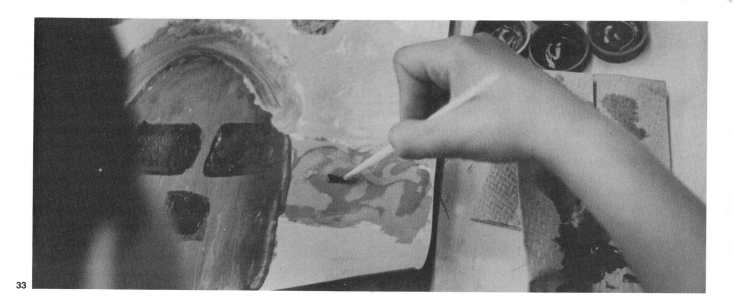

33

missed a particular word had to step down, but when the round was finished they could reenter the contest for the next round. While I watched, I noticed one student standing at the open door, looking in, with both his feet in the hall. He had been reprimanded for misconduct, and directed to stay at the door—in exile, but still under surveillance. Next, in Ms. Humphery's class, I found she had really succumbed to Art Week—or, more accurately, her innate enthusiasm had found an artistic outlet. The pupils were working with diligence at their desks, drawing and painting on the covers of the folders for their projects, each titled, "My Life on an Island." The folders were to hold a variety of completed and planned projects on the "life on an island" theme: an essay, an arithmetic exercise, etc. The project had obviously generated considerable pupil interest (see photo 33).

ABOUT TEACHER EVALUATIONS

On my next visit, I arrived just before 8:30 A.M., on Monday, November 23. I knew Mrs. Culverwell would be meeting this morning with Mrs. Windham and the two other fourth grade teachers. They would discuss her coming evaluation visits to their classrooms. The matter of teacher evaluation is important, and somewhat complex. Thus, it requires some general introduction.

Board procedures require Mrs. Culverwell to make at least one evaluative visit to each teacher's classroom every year. That visit must culminate in the "visitor" completing an evaluation form, and delivering a copy to the teacher. For an enormous number of reasons, this process is followed only very perfunctorily in many Chicago schools—as well as in other American schools. Laypersons may be surprised

that so little scrutiny is given to such an important process as the act of teaching. However, the reasons for such superficiality are manifold:

(1) Most teachers have tenure. Many otherwise busy principals do not see much point in evaluating the work of employees who cannot be fired for incompetence (except in very extreme instances).

(2) Teachers usually receive automatic annual raises, based on their years of service (seniority), and the number of college graduate courses they have taken. Because of such policies, a principal's evaluation—whether good or bad—almost never has any effect on a particular tenured teacher's salary. Furthermore, teachers have very few incentives to treat such evaluations seriously, if they find them disagreeable. They can just tear them up. This situation increases the irrelevance of teacher evaluations.

(3) Principals have an enormous variety of duties beyond visiting classrooms to evaluate teachers. Given the limited effects of evaluation, they prefer to put their energies into apparently more urgent activities.

(4) The responsibility of evaluation is complicated by the comparative privacy surrounding most teachers' activities—carried out in classrooms, removed from simple observation by supervisors and other adults.

(5) Teachers often are isolated from other adults in their work. Because of such patterns of isolation, they are notoriously prone to respond defensively to supervision or support; as a result, principals often find the process of providing necessary supervision to be highly unpleasant—a task even requiring moral courage. Thus,

evaluations tend to be superficial, and perfunctory. It is not uncommon for 75 percent of the teachers in a school to be rated "excellent" by the principal—even though the word "excellent" literally means that the person "excels." It is an oxymoron to say that high proportions of teachers are "excellent."

(6) The concept of "span of control" refers to the number of subordinates one supervisor can effectively oversee. In typical supervisory situations (away from schools), appropriate spans of control range from five to fifteen persons. In other words, most supervisors cannot have the time to effectively supervise (let us say) twenty employees. Each such supervisor will be spread too thin. But, in education, principals are often expected to supervise twenty to forty plus employees. And so Mrs. Culverwell supervises about sixty professionals and subprofessionals at Reilly.

Mrs. Culverwell's Procedure

Despite these barriers, Mrs. Culverwell vigorously exercises her supervisory and teacher support responsibilities. Over the years, she has evolved a relatively elaborate procedure that is also applied by many other effective principals.

Formal, prescheduled classroom visits are only part of a panoply of techniques she applies to obtain elaborate knowledge about teachers' efficacy. Other devices include finding occasions for quick unannounced visits to classrooms; observing classrooms through their open doors, or glass door panels (if doors are closed) as she walks down the hall; reading (or skimming) different documents and reports generated by each teacher's work, or which are required under the procedures applied in Reilly, e.g., lesson plans, samples of student work, materials posted on bulletin boards, report cards delivered to parents (which Mrs. Culverwell examines before they are distributed); observing teacher conduct in the school's many meeting situations; examining records of pupil class attendance and lateness; maintaining informal contacts with parents, pupils, and other teachers; observing pupil conduct outside the classroom (as they move through the halls, or in assemblies); and keeping track of pupils' scores on standardized tests.

Mrs. Culverwell makes a determined and largely successful effort to carefully choose the staff members regularly assigned to Reilly. If she has a vacancy, and a teacher employed elsewhere in the system asks to be transferred in, part of her screening process may include visiting the teacher at his/her present school, and observing his/her classroom work.

Teachers at Reilly are required to apply certain uniform procedures, which tend to (1) enhance the quality of their instruction, and (2) make it less likely that they will err in their teaching, e.g., school policies about amounts of homework, the number of grades pupils must earn each marking period, and lesson plans that are subject to review by the principal.

Teachers are assigned to work in committees with others teaching a similar grade level or subject matter. Committee responsibilities are taken seriously, and Mrs. Culverwell monitors the work of the committees. Involvement in committees helps teachers improve their skills and provides them with incentives to stay professionally informed.

Mrs. Culverwell has considerable moral courage. She is polite, soft spoken, and solicitous. However, any careful observer can recognize that she sees herself as personally responsible for the overall welfare of the school. She strongly resists attempts to undercut her authority and responsibility. Furthermore, her evident dedication gives her an "edge" in many potential conflicts. The respect she has earned makes staff members disposed to do what she recommends.

Mrs. Culverwell is skilled in developing alliances and supporters and using established procedures to maintain her authority. Potential resisters are deterred from confronting someone with such a strong power base. Furthermore, in her evaluations, she assumes she will find most teacher practices deserving of praise, and she provides that praise. But there will also be occasions for correction. Then, she assumes that most teachers who make mistakes are open to appropriate correction. Finally, teachers who are reluctant to change can often be persuaded or compelled to improve, or leave the school.

Many elements of the systems of teacher supervision currently applied are distressing: it is unrealistic to have one principal supervise sixty people; the existing tenure provisions are probably too restrictive; and, if good principals must have moral courage—a rare quality—we will have too many inadequate principals. Of course, it is possible to conceptualize many promising improvements in the current supervision system. However, each current inefficiency satisfies the needs of important existing interest groups. Thus, while many informed persons and groups decry the situation, they also often strongly resist particular efforts to correct the status quo. Now that we have some perspective, let us return to Mrs. Culverwell meeting in her office with the fourth grade teachers.

The Meetings

Mrs. Culverwell gave each teacher a tabulation. It listed the reading score improvement (over the year) of all of last year's fourth grade pupils, and the entry level scores of this year's fourth graders. The data for these tabulations was developed by Mrs. DePaul, the school's reading specialist, from the school's records of pupils' annual reading tests. Mrs. Culverwell said that last year's performance for the grade, as a whole, was unsatisfactory. This year she hoped that the current fourth graders' performance would show some improvement. She told the teachers that they should each examine, in their own records, their particular class's test score data, and identify the patterns of reading scores for their class, i.e., what proportion of their pupils were reading below, at, or above grade levels.

Mrs. Culverwell also asked the teachers to articulate, on their forms, what general teaching strategy was appropriate for their classes, on the basis of their scores. In particular, she was concerned with the development of two or more "reading groups" for each class. In such groups, pupils with about the same reading levels would receive focused instruction.

After adding the required information, the teachers were to return their sheet to Mrs. Culverwell. Each returned sheet should include the teacher's recommendations of a date and time for a class visit by Mrs. Culverwell.

Mrs. Culverwell then went on to discuss, with the teachers, different teaching tactics that might improve the grade's performance, which was largely defined as increasing pupil scores on various standardized tests. One particular direction dealt with the subject matter presented in social science.

The idea of a group meeting to start the evaluation is unusual, and interesting. (The final evaluation meeting for each teacher will be one-to-one.) In part, such group meetings save Mrs. Culverwell's time; the starting message is the same for most teachers at the same grade level. Furthermore, she undoubtedly wants to mobilize group support and pressure to advance the school's goals. And, since all teachers at the grade were given the same information, they will be encouraged to work together to meet the group challenge. Finally, experts in pupil testing emphasize that the validity of groups of test scores increases greatly if the scores generated by pupils in several classes at the same level are merged. Conversely, it is often a statistical error to weight one teacher's performance in terms of the test score shifts in his/her one class. By merging the scores together, Mrs. Culverwell moderated such criticisms.

THE DEATH OF THE MAYOR

On Friday, November 27, Harold Washington, the Mayor of Chicago (and its first black mayor), died of a sudden heart attack. Over the succeeding weekend, it was announced that the Chicago public schools would only meet briefly on Monday. Pupils would then be sent home from schools, to symbolically participate in the widespread mourning. When

I arrived at the school at 8:30 on Monday, I noticed the school flag at half mast.

Before classes began, it was announced that there would be a schoolwide faculty meeting in the library at 8:45. While the teachers waited patiently at the library tables, I noticed Mrs. Culverwell arrive at one library door and stop briefly to confer with several teachers. The group included Mrs. Ebner, whose eighth grade class was practiced in singing under her leadership, and Mrs. DePaul, who usually played the piano during assemblies.

Mrs. Culverwell then announced to the teachers the plans for a memorial assembly for the Mayor, to be held a few minutes after school began. Several students, recruited from the Student Council by Miss Nicks, would make memorial remarks, Mrs. Culverwell would deliver an adult appreciation, and Mrs. Ebner's choir would perform. Kindergarten through third grades would remain in their classes during the assembly—and engage in "appropriate activities"—and the whole school would be dismissed after the assembly.

As the library meeting broke up, I went to the school doorway, to watch the entering pupils. They seemed to be unusually somber (see photo 34).

At the assembly, things went as planned. Mrs. Culverwell delivered her brief and focused speech. A large photograph of Mayor Washington, hung with black cloth, sat on an easel on the stage. Mrs. Ebner's pupils sang the "Battle Hymn of the Republic." The Student Council President and Vice President made brief remarks, and (presumably because the Student Council officers were white) a third student, a black girl from an upper grade, also offered some observations from the podium. At one point, I visited Mrs. Estes' class, to see what "appropriate activities" were underway. She had directed each of the pupils to draw and color a picture of what the Mayor's death signified to them and the city. She told them that they would later be asked to explain their drawings to their classmates. At the end of the assembly, the pupils were dismissed for the day.

It seemed the school had done a good job of adapting to an unusual challenge.

A CHILD AT RISK

One assembly incident was not strictly planned. During the ceremony, I noticed Miss Swiatek come into the auditorium with a pupil beside her. She directed him to sit with his class. Mrs. Culverwell then came over and chatted briefly with Miss Swiatek. After talking with Mrs. Culverwell, Miss Swiatek took the pupil, and led him out of the assembly. After the assembly was dismissed, I noticed Miss Swiatek standing beside the pupil at a desk in the school office, overseeing his writing out some statement.

Several days later, Miss Swiatek gave me the background

34

on the incident. The pupil was in seventh grade. He had a long history of poor schoolwork, and was a recurrent discipline problem. On the day of the assembly, he had gotten into a sharp dispute with the substitute teacher in his class and had threatened her physically. Mrs. Culverwell had asked Miss Swiatek to remove the boy from the assembly; she did not want him sitting with his classmates until the matter had been formally handled.

The statement he was writing out in the office was his description of the dispute. The school often had students write out statements about discipline incidents, and had found they were usually truthful and informative. The statements were often of use in later discussions with parents.

Miss Swiatek had previously carried out several efforts to moderate the boy's difficulties—including recruiting her sister to serve as a volunteer tutor for him. But the boy had not been able to mobilize himself enough to take advantage of the help. Furthermore, his family situation was very difficult, e.g., a single parent at home, plus alcoholism. Basically, he was a child "at risk." I mused at the idea of an assistant principal who went around recruiting her sister to tutor such exposed pupils. I had never heard of any such job description. From my other contacts with Miss Swiatek, I know what she would say if I asked her about that matter. "One just doesn't simply give up on a thirteen year old. We have to lose in some circumstances, but there is no excuse for not giving a good try."

35

IN CLASSROOMS

On Tuesday, December 1, I began in Mrs. Canepa's class at about 9:05. Shortly after class opened, Miss Nicks, the science teacher, came in. With Mrs. Canepa's permission, she made a few remarks to the class. She reminded them, in strong terms, that when they came to her science class later in the day, they should be sure to bring with them their materials for their science fair projects. She did not want them to leave the supplies in another class, and have to ask permission to return and pick them up. Essentially, Miss Nicks worked hard at maintaining the attention of her pupils. The next day, in the afternoon, I visited Ms. Humphery's room. Her students were presenting their individual science projects. Ms. Humphery was judging which ones should be passed on to the schoolwide science fair. The presentations were also a form of practice, since fair participants had to orally explain their projects to fair visitors and judges. One of her pupils, Ishmael, whom we have already met, had some difficulties with his display. Ms. Humphery became vigorously engaged in helping him.

Mrs. Lucas' class was deeply involved in constructing paper Santa Claus figures (see photo 35). The figures were composed of pieces of paper and cotton which the students had to assemble and paste together. Mrs. Lucas mentioned to me that over 1,000 separate parts were handed out to the students for assembly. She had created the parts in the evening at home. Mrs. Lucas saw such projects as having a variety of benefits: they gave pupils practice in manipulating tools (scissors, glue); displaying patience and discipline; and following oral directions.

At 8:30, on Friday, December 4, I attended the monthly

steering committee meeting. The meeting has an agenda of sixteen subtopics (see photo 36). The committee was comprised of Mrs. Culverwell, Miss Swiatek, and a teacher representing each of the three grade levels. In particular, the adopt-a-school program was given as careful a coverage as time allowed.

Report cards were to be delivered to parents on Wednesday afternoon, December 9. Mrs. Culverwell stamped her name on all cards, and she regularly examined them all before delivery. In particular, she noted the cards with especially good or bad marks for conduct or academics, and wrote brief words of praise or caution on them. This amounted to about 10 percent of the cards. On all of the other cards, she simply stamped a star beside her name, or sometimes put in a word or two.

Her "oversight" served a variety of purposes: it helped her notice the exceptionally good and bad pupils in the school; gave her a feel of the teachers' grading patterns; and provided pupils with additional incentives to engage in good behavior. She started receiving the completed cards from her teachers on the afternoon of December 4.

ATTENDANCE

I visited the school on the morning of Tuesday, December 8. In the hall, Miss Swiatek called my attention to the attendance banner, which Reilly had just earned for its best-in-the-district attendance in November. She also remarked on the materials on the attendance bulletin board, across the hall from the banner.

36

37

One chart included a tabulation of each month's pupil attendance rate for the current schoolyear for each Reilly class. Miss Swiatek had posted, beside the chart, a newspaper clipping about a boy from Arkansas. He had graduated from high school after completing a record of perfect attendance for all of his twelve years of school. The article said that he had deliberately set this goal while attending elementary school. Miss Swiatek especially emphasized the boy's motto, which was quoted in the article. It was set in bold type on the bulletin board: "If you work hard enough at something—you will achieve your goal."

The matter of attendance deserves some explicit attention. During the previous year Reilly had won the district's prize as the school with the best attendance record. The school

38

hoped to do the same this year. The pupils were interested in the progress of this contest; I have occasionally seen them examining their school and class standing on the tabulation. Furthermore, on the outside door of each classroom was listed the names of students in that class who had perfect attendance last month. And one Friday afternoon each month, the pupils who had achieved perfect attendance were taken to a movie in the auditorium. Separate films were provided for the upper and lower grades.

Of course, the faculty realize that attendance is important—pupils can't learn lessons unless they are in school. But the faculty also generally believe in the character-building value of attendance: it is good for young people to develop diligence and persistence. Furthermore, even if students are not academic stars, they can all take some pride in the display of good attendance. Thus, stressing attendance is a way of giving every pupil a share in helping the school.

Miss Swiatek's enthusiasm touches on a final point. People who lead and shape children should be able to understand, and sometimes share, "childish" emotions. Despite what the boy said in the clipping, all goals are not achievable—and Miss Swiatek knows that. But it is good for children when adults transmit such optimistic messages to them with intensity and sincerity; and point them toward difficult but achievable goals.

THE SCIENCE FAIR

I then went up to see the science fair finals. About fifty projects were exhibited in the gym. Across the side of the gym, a series of photos were hanging from a line—pictures of the winning pupils of all Reilly science fairs since 1980. While the exhibits were displayed, each class in the school came to briefly visit the show and appreciate the contributions of their peers. Exhibitors were identified by the ribbons they wore.

Exhibitors were busy explaining their creations to visiting pupils. In addition, a team of judges, comprised of two Reilly teachers, and Mr. Jerry Hays, a science-curriculum consultant from the board, identified the final winners (see photo 37). When I left the building at the end of the day, a new poster was conspicuously mounted at the main school door. It displayed the names and photographs of the winning exhibitors, plus the titles of their exhibits. As usual, the school had moved quickly to reinforce desirable behavior.

REPORT CARDS

The next day was report card day. Pupils only attended school for the morning. Parents were strongly urged (at their convenience) to come into the school that day to receive the first card. Teachers were required to be present for the whole day, from 8:30 A.M. until 7:00 P.M., to allow for parents' job responsibilities. The process is designed to encourage teacher-parent communication to advance pupil learning (see photo 38). The PTA maintained a table at a central point on the first-floor hall, to aid its recruiting. All of the teachers had made arrangements to generally display the work of their pupils, and many of the teachers took different measures to heighten the attractiveness of their classrooms (see photo 39). Such measures were more than "public relations." They said to the parents (and to their children, too) that parents were special people, and should receive special courtesies. The science fair exhibits were also left up for parents to examine. No notable problems came to my attention in connection with the visits.

39

40

At 3:30 in the afternoon, the teachers suspended their parent meetings and took a break in the teacher's lounge — they still had several long hours ahead. During the break, Mrs. Kane, and several other PTA mothers who had been in the school through the day, joined the group. The mothers then announced that the PTA was immediately donating a microwave oven to the lounge in recognition of the fine support the teachers had given the PTA recruiting campaign — and as a general sign of appreciation. The teachers were pleased. They responded by singing "For They Are Jolly Good Mothers." Then Mrs. Fotos, the co-chair of the social committee, announced that at the final end of the day (or evening), some faculty were gathering at a neighborhood restaurant for a late dinner. All were invited to come along.

The faculty then returned to their classrooms and more meetings.

IN THE OFFICE

I entered the school office on the morning of December 14. I was surprised to see Mrs. Tamez seated at a desk, performing clerical work. I had seen her around the school since her termination; she routinely worked as a volunteer on Fridays. But this was Monday. I discovered that Mrs. Culverwell had been able to hire her back full-time — via a device I would have to ask about.

I visited Mrs. Culverwell's office, to pose an inquiry. She was seriously engaged in a discussion with Miss Swiatek. It seems Miss Swiatek while acting as counsellor/disciplinarian, had suspended an unruly pupil, but Mrs. Culverwell asked if the appropriate procedures had been followed. It was evident that not all the "t's" had been crossed, or the "i's" dotted. Miss Swiatek kept her cool in the face of a tacit reprimand. But no one could believe the conversation pleased her (see photo 40).

Mrs. Culverwell asked, "Why did you do this without checking with me?" Miss Swiatek replied, "This happened that day last week, when we were forced to be doing six things at once. I had to make a fast decision." The charged conversation then became further complicated: several teachers began entering Mrs. Culverwell's office, to have the group meeting before individual classroom visits.

As the teachers came in, Mrs. Culverwell, in a calm but firm voice, told Miss Swiatek to call the parent; tell her that an incorrect procedure had been followed, and the suspension was withdrawn. Miss Swiatek indicated acquiescence, and left the room. The teachers' meeting then began. I do not know if any teachers understood what was happening as they entered, but some of them might have made good guesses.

The incident apparently conflicts with one popular principle of management: make rebukes private. It also seems to conflict with Mrs. Culverwell's general aura of tact and goodwill. But the incident is not completely inconsistent with Mrs. Culverwell's managerial principles. Later in this text, we will see at least one equivalent incident involving another school employee. Furthermore, in private discussions, Mrs. Culverwell characterized herself to me as sometimes quite outspoken. The description seems accurate. But it has broader implications.

CARVING OUT AUTHORITY

Commentators have contended that many school principals, like Mrs. Culverwell, are relatively powerless. They cannot give raises to their more competent workers and, conversely, marginal employees receive the same pay as the best workers. True, Mrs. Culverwell has certain "forms" of authority: she evaluates each employee annually, and can supposedly initiate discharge proceedings. But the constraints on such authority are immense. This discrepancy between the formal and actual authority of Mrs. Culverwell—and many other principals—is a source of complication.

Effective principals learn to cultivate real authority beneath this umbrella of ambiguity. Different able principals use different tactics to attain this end. One basic source of Mrs. Culverwell's authority is her high level of moral courage. The concept of moral courage is important and warrants explication. The word "courage" means a disposi-

tion to act despite the existence of real causes for fear. But courage can be displayed in different circumstances. Thus, there can be physical courage—acting despite the appropriate fear of physical injury, pain, or even death. In contrast, moral courage means acting to overcome emotional resistance in order to attain a morally correct end. Moral courage may, but need not, also encompass physical courage. Or moral courage may simply mean overcoming hostility, or the anger of others, but not necessarily risking physical danger. In other words, one may display physical courage for bad or selfish ends—for instance, there can be a brave robber. But people can only practice moral courage when they act for moral or unselfish ends, i.e., not to get a raise or increase their own power, but essentially to see the right thing is done.

Especially in schools, persons who display moral courage can attain considerable authority. Parents and school staff themselves are already acting in their roles for partly moral reasons. Few people bear children or become teachers to become rich or attain great power, and so a designated leader who shows her assertions are largely motivated by moral factors can acquire considerable popular support. People around schools want such leaders. They feel better when they are regularly reminded of the critical moral components of their work, especially when the reminder comes from someone they see as sincere. Another virtue of moral courage, or leadership, is that it encourages persons working under a moral leader to mimic such important traits in their own conduct. It seemed to me that moral leadership was common among Reilly faculty, e.g., Miss Swiatek's dedication.

Mrs. Culverwell partly displays her moral leadership in her willingness to engage in firm, tactful, or even public confrontations when necessary. Due to a mix of judgment and experience, she usually identifies incidents where such confrontations are hard to resist. For instance, Miss Swiatek never said her conduct was correct; she simply asked to be excused. And Mrs. Culverwell, in effect, said her mistake was so serious that she would not back her up.

The essentially public nature of this criticism—whether due to deliberation or coincidence—had another implication. It both added to its impact, and warned witnesses to avoid equivalent mistakes. In sum, Mrs. Culverwell does not have much formal power. However, she has developed a body of substantial authority, partly because she has the courage and wisdom to use her status to deliver justified public criticisms—or to put people in fear of such criticisms. I should also emphasize that she did not bear grudges; her reprimands did not dispose her to dismiss people's positive achievements. Indeed, 75 percent or more of her public evaluative remarks were words of praise.

41

IN CLASSROOMS

As classes began, I visited Mrs. Lucas. Her teaching commenced with the day's "story": the sentence(s) appropriate for the day. This procedure was also applied in Mrs. Estes' first grade class. Students were expected to read and write out the sentence(s) written on the board. Mrs. Lucas' sentence was "The sun was up." The sentence was at about the level of the first grade (see photo 41). Some of Mrs. Lucas' students had difficulty with the exercise.

I returned to Mrs. Culverwell's office, and found out about Mrs. Tamez's return. The parents of certain students in the school, e.g., some Poles, and Humong tribespeople, might be officially classified as "refugees" under a federal program providing funds for students from such families. Such funds were allocated to the Chicago system, delivered to the board, and redistributed to local schools. Mrs. Culverwell asked the staff members managing the program to allocate some funds to Reilly so that she could rehire Mrs. Tamez to work with the refugee children.

The response was inconclusive. She followed up with a strong letter, tacitly even implying the funds were "fraudulently" withheld. She mentioned about calling the matter to the attention of parent and community groups. The staff relented, and released funds for her to rehire Mrs. Tamez. Formally, Mrs. Tamez's new assignment is to work with

"refugees." The return of Mrs. Tamez was a help to the school, a reward to a competent employee, and a message to all staff that their leader was loyal and effective.

In the afternoon, I dropped by the auditorium. Christmas preparations were in progress. Different classes, one at a time, were entering the auditorium and practicing the particular song(s) each would sing at the Christmas assembly. In all cases, but especially with the younger grades, equal emphasis was placed on group movement (into the auditorium and on and off stage) and the performance of songs. The aim was to put the pupils on their "best behavior." There was incidentally an assumption that without practice, apparently simple things might go quite wrong. Both children and teachers treated the activities seriously.

Mrs. Culverwell, at the end of the day, was busy reviewing teachers' lesson plans and grade books. These were delivered by teachers to her monthly. When she returned them, she often included her comments and suggestions. The documents were important instruments for the supervision and support of teachers. The plans showed what the teachers expected to cover daily, the ways they proposed to teach, and how they would evaluate pupils' learning. Furthermore, each day's plan was meant to be integrated into a vision of what is to be covered throughout the year, and at what rate instruction should move. (Mrs. Culverwell understands that teachers may occasionally need to vary or revise the presentation of planned material; however, while such variations can sometimes be acceptable, it is not acceptable to go in and teach without a plan.) The grade books showed the grades the teachers had periodically entered to measure each pupil's learning in each subject.

From the documents, Mrs. Culverwell could see whether teachers had sound plans. The grade books showed if that procedure was applied, and if students were apparently being successful.

It is theoretically possible for a teacher to "fake" the plan and grade book; to put one thing on paper, and act differently in class. However, (1) such faking is difficult to do if other, complementary forms of supervision are also applied, and (2) if a teacher had devised a plausible written plan and system of examination, it may be easier to actually carry it out, compared to attempting an exercise in fakery.

Of course, before her reviews, Mrs. Culverwell can make informed estimates about whose plans will probably be sound, and whose need follow-up. But even the established staff recognize that the principal may pay attention to their planning. Mrs. Culverwell can also identify good ideas being tried by her able teachers, and pass them on to other staff members.

From my experience among Chicago area schools, I estimate that Mrs. Culverwell's process of plan examination is in the top 20 percent in rigor applied. In many schools, lesson plan examination by principals or other supervisors is superficial. Various justifications are provided for such nonexamination, e.g., teachers do not always follow their plans, or a focus on plan examination stifles teacher creativity. The merits of these contentions are problematic. One must also recognize that examining lesson plans involves work for supervisors; many teachers do not like to develop clear written plans, or have their teaching analyzed and evaluated; and some supervisors are poorly skilled at examining such documents.

THE SUBSTANCE ABUSE MEETING

On Tuesday, December 15, a PTA meeting on substance abuse was held in the auditorium. The meeting was also scheduled as an assembly for seventh and eighth grade pupils. It had been organized by Mrs. Nelson, the PTA program chair. Essentially, the program presented three speakers—a young white woman, a young black male, and an older black woman. They were all former abusers, now associated with a rehabilitation program. About seven parents attended the program; most adults are not free on weekday mornings. But student interest in the presentations was palpable (see photo 42). And probably the program was aimed at students more than adults.

42

43

The speakers recited vivid, terrible stories about their declines into addiction—to drugs and/or alcohol—and their gradual and intermittent rehabilitation. Phrases were uttered such as, "I was a human garbage can," "I was sent into mandatory drug rehabilitation in twenty-five separate criminal cases," and "I am still getting bills for emergency service in overdose incidents, when I can't even remember the incidents" (see photo 43). (Mrs. Nelson is sitting behind the table, on the left.)

Technically, it is not easy to accurately evaluate the effects of such "testimonial" presentations. Do they really discourage pupils from using drugs? It is said that, in some circumstances, such activities can do as much to glamorize drugs as to warn pupils off. But, as a rule of thumb, we should assume people are motivated by the evident principles derived from the conduct of others. Applying this rule, the sincere warnings underlying the testimonies probably had a beneficial effect on the students.

Many schools would be reluctant to bring such strong materials before a student audience, despite their essentially constructive content. One reason for the reluctance would be the fear of parent complaints. PTA sponsorship obviously muted such potential protests. The presentation was an ingenious instance of parent/school cooperation.

On Friday, December 10, the Polish bilingual pupils were to sing Christmas carols in the school. I arrived with mild curiosity. The affair was extremely impressive (see photo 44). The older Polish boys had built a model church for the occasion. The model, on a platform, was carried aloft by several boys, leading a procession of carollers. The whole group was led by a boy carrying a star. Many of the carollers were girls, dressed in (apparently) native Polish costumes (see photo 45). They proceeded throughout the school, singing carols in Polish. A group of pleased Polish parents, largely mothers, followed the procession, which was accompanied by the pupils' teachers. As the procession came outside each non-Polish classroom, the teachers brought their classes out for the occasion. The pupils were evidently pleased by the display and singing.

The lovely occasion clearly absorbed a body of school—as well as family—resources. It leads to an obvious question: Is it educationally sound for a school to encourage such activities, or should they be left to churches, and other public agencies? Furthermore, as we will see again, Reilly is sympathetic to putting time in such "spectacular" activities. Is this wise?

Most humans take a delight in spectacle, and in aesthetic display and participation. Even people with mediocre talent can participate in such events and make appropriate contributions, depending on how the activities are designed. Furthermore, the activities build community, and articulate group values. In an ethnically disparate school like Reilly, the carolling displayed Polish traditions and let the Poles provide their "gift" to the whole institution. Finally, such group aesthetic activities are a realistic test of organizational and discipline structure of a school. Carrying out the carolling is a demonstration of a school's efficacy. At least one reason some schools avoid such activities is that they cannot handle the planning, or maintain necessary order.

I know of some well-reputed (often private secular) schools in the Chicago area that do not encourage such activities. They would presumably decry them as a waste of academic time, and as being of little intellectual content. Unfortunately, it is also my impression that too often such schools, despite the talents of their carefully screened pupils, are relatively cold institutions. They are also afflicted with high levels of pupil selfishness, loneliness, and egocentricity.

I visited the office about 1 P.M. on Tuesday, December 22. Mrs. Culverwell was having a warm conversation with Ralph, the building engineer. He was being transferred to another school, and was saying goodbye. He mentioned that he had served in twenty-three different Chicago schools during his career. I asked him how Reilly compared to those other schools. He said it rated at or near the top. I asked him why he said that.

45

46

He replied with emphasis, "Nice people. Just nice people." The photo (see photo 46) shows Ralph (on the right) talking with two of his four assistants, in the school boiler room.

To put Ralph's point more expansively: (1) Mrs. Culverwell is a nice person, (2) she knows what conduct translates into being nice, (3) she works hard to hire nice people as staff members, (4) she tries to keep nice people on her staff, and cause the not-nice-ones to change or leave, and (5) she manages the school so that "niceness" is encouraged and "meanness" is discouraged. And the school's stress on niceness applies to both pupils and staff.

When I visited the auditorium, I found some classes still conducting final practices for tomorrow's Christmas Assembly for parents. Mrs. Ebner, an eighth grade teacher, told her pupils, "I don't care tomorrow if every other student in the place is noisy. You will be quiet."

In Ms. Humphery's room, preparations were underway for tomorrow's class party—after the assembly. A long list had been prepared, with student involvement, of the food and games to be brought by designated pupils. Ms. Humphery also mentioned to me that she had made arrangements so that no pupils were left out in the in-class gift exchanges that would occur at the party.

When I visited Mrs. Lucas' class near the end of the afternoon, I found her trying to teach the children the difference between the concepts of "need" and "want"—a relevant issue around Christmas time. Mrs. Barreto too was assisting her as translator. Her enthusiasm was attractive, but I wondered if the complex lesson had gone home (see photo 47).

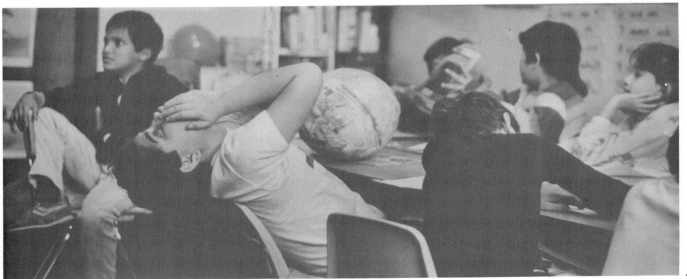

47

48

PARTY DAY

The next day, Wednesday, December 23, was the last school day before Christmas. I dropped by the auditorium at about 9:20—the Parents' Assembly was set for 9:30. (Two days back, the pupils had presented their same performances to each other at the pupils' Christmas Assembly, in a sort of final rehearsal.) About 200 parents were already seated. Male/female proportions were 70/30. At 9:30, Mrs. Culverwell stepped to the podium to commence the occasion. The color guards trooped in. By this time, all of the seats were filled, and a number of parents were standing in the back. Each of the twenty classrooms of regular students in the school presented a separate "number" on the stage,

under the direction of their individual teachers. All of the classes were dressed relatively formally (see photo 48).

As one would expect, the parents were enormously pleased—"You sounded real good out there, sweetie." The songs presented included "Little Lord Jesus," "Jolly Old Saint Nick," "Santa Claus Is Coming to Town," "Adeste Fideles" (in Latin), "I'll Be Home for Christmas," and "O Holy Night," plus a Polish and a Spanish carol, each of undoubtedly religious origins. Most of the songs were chosen from a booklet of Christmas songs, supplied as an advertising device by an insurance company. They were certainly chosen because the teachers knew and liked them, felt they were easy to teach, and thought the parents and pupils would like them too.

Part of the reason the songs were affecting was because of their substantial religious elements. Technically, if some citizen brought suit to prohibit the future singing of such songs in the Reilly school, or in the Chicago system—arguing that it is in conflict with the separation of church and state—he/she would probably win. I say "probably" because the matter could be affected by a variety of circumstances.

In some—probably quite a few—communities, such in-school Christmas presentations have been abandoned because of the legal and community conflicts engendered. One source of such conflicts is the tremendous leverage dissatisfied individuals and small groups have been given by recent court decisions. Even if all of the Reilly parents were pleased by the Christmas assembly, any citizen (assisted by the ACLU?) could probably get the activity enjoined. The partial abandonment of such presentations throughout America—and the "sterilization" of other holiday celebrations—means that one powerful tool for engendering a sense of community around public schools has been discarded. We should also recognize that the whole Polish student carolling ceremony could also be prohibited. The Polish hymns undoubtedly had a religious content, and the students sung them partly to express beliefs.

Of course, the matter is enormously complicated. One Jewish friend of mine recalls attending Chicago public schools and being required to participate in ceremonies like those at Reilly. He remembers his awkwardness and discomfiture.

Conversely, I had a graduate student, an Hassidic Jew—with a beard, black hat, and frock coat. He wrote a thoughtful paper, about his former public elementary school principal who forced all pupils to sing Christmas hymns. The Hassidim (now at age thirty-five) looks back on the principal as a kind man of principle and determination, and an admirable educator. (Of course, the young Hassidic boy was more affected by the "sing the hymn" decree than was my Jewish friend. To the Hassidim, the requirement was semi-traumatic.) The final irony is that my "Jewish" friend, who still objects to carolling, is only a mildly observant Jew. The Hassidim, who is obviously highly devout, sees his carolling incident as the inevitable concomitant of any serious religious belief.

The assembly took about one and a half hours. Later in the afternoon, I visited throughout the school. Parties were in progress in each class. In Mrs. Windham's room, juice, cookies, and other goodies were freely available, and many children were engaged in board games (see photo 49).

In the gym, a dance—open to the seventh and eighth

49

50

grades—was underway. Music was supplied by a phonograph. Teachers circulated as chaperones, but they had little to do. Most of the boys, and many of the girls, found dancing too uncomfortable. They sat things out as wallflowers (see photo 50). But the faculty saw such "dances" as foster-

ing a sound developmental process—by seventh and eighth grade, it is time for boys and girls to begin thinking about, and practicing, responsible intermixing.

After exchanging season's greetings with my hosts, I left everybody to enjoy their break until January 4, next year.

Chapter Five

BACK TO WORK

I'm the Floor

I'm the floor in the room, and I'm tired of getting stepped on. After all its ruining my new suit. I wish I could be the ceiling, but I'm just an old classroom floor.

(From a variety of brief literary exercises published in the school creative writing paper, Sparkles.*)*

WHEN school resumed on Monday, January 4, I visited Mrs. Lucas' class at about 11:15. Many of her pupils were wearing jackets. It was cold outside, the building had been shut down for almost two weeks, and the room was usually not very warm anyway. There was a back-to-business atmosphere, though some decorations were still displayed. Mrs. Lucas was taking the students through a series of drills, to teach the concepts "near" and "far," and "under" and "over" (see photo 51). She held a card out with one of these words written in English. Particular students were then asked to move some designated object into the appropriate locations, e.g., either near or far. The students were being taught via a variety of "modalities." They saw the written word, heard it spoken, were asked to act it out, and also saw each other in such acting.

By Tuesday, January 5, cold weather was really setting in. Mrs. Windham announced in her class, at 9:05, that fifteen students were absent, obviously due to the weather. The students released an audible groan: they had enthusiastically enlisted in Mrs. Windham's (and the school's) attendance campaign, and were disappointed at the class's poor showing.

THE BULLETIN BOARD

When I entered the school the next day, there was an elaborate display on the bulletin board immediately outside the office. The display was keyed to the forthcoming celebrations of Washington's and Lincoln's Birthdays. It had been developed under the leadership of Miss Knott, the librarian.

Each class was scheduled for a certain amount of library time. Miss Knott usually applied that time for various book-related assignments. Thus, some fourth and fifth grade pupils developed the essays posted on the board as a result of her assignments. One typical essay by Ludmilla Jegier, a pupil of Mrs. Windham's (see photo 52), went as follows (the text is exact, including malapropisms):

Work Hard

If you work hard you might be a president one day. I try and work hard at everything I do. When I get home from school, I work hard. I throw out garbage, wash the dishes, and when I clean the house, I try to do my best. When I do my homework I work as hard as I can, and try not to mess up.

Abraham Lincoln always worked hard. He was always a good leader and a good follower. He was always honest, and he helped people out. The same with George Washington. In order to be president you always had to work hard. That was one of the important things about being president. All people that have careers work hard too. They are: teachers, lawyers, nurses, doctors, dentists, veterinarians, machine workers. There are a lot of careers that people work hard in. Working hard is important to everybody.

The other essays had titles such as "Be a Learner," "Be Fair," and "Be Patriotic."

Bulletin boards, in general, were a significant element of the school. There were about twenty to twenty-five boards in the corridors, spread throughout all floors. Each was redecorated about five times a year, according to a published schedule. Each board, or each specific change (in some "major" boards), was assigned to an identified teacher and class. Usually, the room number of the class responsible was publicly noted on the board. An implicit competition—or at least the desire to look one's best in public—affected the process of decoration. Teachers had discretion in their designs. They chose diverse themes: pupils' class work, aesthetic creations, and seasonal and holiday topics. The boards emphasized the values of the school.

51

The boards were part of the school's environment. And the school staff had an acute perception of the meaning of that important word and concept. The Reilly environment was comprised of what the staff, pupils, and parents saw and heard:

- what was on bulletin boards
- what activities were prominently announced (like the Science Fair winners) or conspicuously counted (like each class's score in the attendance contest)
- how teachers and pupils dressed
- what words people used to express what ideas
- what symbols and activities were given priority (e.g., saluting the flag, keeping assemblies orderly, getting work done on time, keeping the premises neat and clean, helping younger students)
- what ideas and values were emphasized
- what sorts of conduct were expected from students and staff

Before classes, I overheard an incidental conservation between Miss Nicks and Ms. Humphery. They were commiserating with each other about paperwork responsibilities. They each observed that they planned to stay over after school today to finish their paperwork, so they would not have to take more work home.

In the office, a conversation with Miss Swiatek drifted onto personal values. It enriched my understanding of both her values, and many of the values pervading Reilly. She described some of the home situations of pupils she dealt with as counsellor and disciplinarian. Her remarks were pervaded with compassion. But she also was indignant at the uncaring emptiness of many parents, which was manifested in such forms as alcoholism, out-of-wedlock children, and child abuse. To her, many parents were not meeting their responsibilities towards their children. Thus, they were often reluctant to come to school and talk over their children's obvious problems, or even to respond to Miss Swiatek's phone calls.

She fully realized the justifications that might be offered for such apparent indifference, e.g., the parents' neuroses, the other urgent problems confronting them, their embarrassment at their apparent inadequacy. But Miss Swiatek believed in personal responsibility. She felt that many of these excuses smacked of self-indulgence. If someone is an alcoholic or drug addict, or has four out-of-wedlock children, he or she must accept the responsibility (and guilt) associated with such choices. She also evinced her own considerable dedication to "duty."

52

We talked about the doctoral degree she was pursuing. The degree would only moderately increase her pay. Furthermore, attaining the degree would probably not help her advancement. After thirty-five years of school experience, her promotion prospects were only modest. When asked about her motives for taking her doctorate, she replied, "I have a sort of sense of religious dedication, and believe we all have a duty to keep learning throughout our lives."

The Reilly faculty, in general, had high aspirations for themselves as educators, and for what the school could and should do. Remember the show of hands in the library, where the majority of the faculty said they believed their students could achieve national norms? I am sure Miss Swiatek was one of those voting for high aspirations. Presumably, the teachers also believed that, if they should not make excuses for themselves, it was also fair for them to hold significant expectations for those around them, i.e., pupils and parents. Despite the handicaps confronting many parents, the teachers generally believed that all parents should and could provide their children with appropriate emotional support and attention.

And yet the teachers' aspirations were not quite unrealistic. The environment was pretty much under the faculty's control. They did work together to make the school a supportive and benign place. They formed, in effect, a semi-utopian community. Many of the school's families were obviously sympathetic to the faculty's goals—for example, the active PTA members. And other families were neutral. But some of the families (and other elements in the external environment), it might seem, actively opposed their aspirations. The teachers responded to such resistance with efforts at persuasion, and eventually tacit hostility and overt criticism.

THE STAFFING

At nine on the morning of Wednesday, January 6, I went to a Reilly "staffing." Such meetings were a by-product of Reilly's special education program. A requirement of such programs—established by the governing federal law—was that students assigned to special education, or considered for assignment, must be evaluated by a multidisciplinary team. For instance, all of Mrs. Lucas' pupils were staffed before being assigned, and would periodically be reevaluated by a somewhat abbreviated staffing.

The staffing team included all persons in the school working closely with the child, plus other appropriate school system professionals, and the child's parent(s). The staffing I attended, concerned with one pupil, lasted about an hour and forty-five minutes. Throughout most of it, nine people were present, including the classroom teacher, a psychologist, the child's speech therapist Miss Bressler, Mrs. Culverwell, Miss Swiatek in her role as guidance counsellor, a social worker, a nurse, and the child's mother.

Some members at the staffing were full-time faculty at Reilly, while others worked from the district office. Before the staffing, several of the professionals concerned had individually examined the child from their different perspectives, interviewed her mother, and generated and circulated appropriate reports.

The quality of staffings varies widely among schools, regarding the degree of preparation involved and the discourse conducted. In some schools, principals do not even significantly participate. It seemed the one I witnessed at Reilly was highly professional, and I am certain (from many other things I have seen and heard) that this one was similar to other Reilly staffings. Another matter reinforcing my opinion is the high regard the Chicago system holds for Mrs. Culverwell in the area of special education: she was one of two elementary school principals (out of 490 such principals) appointed to a systemwide committee to advise the system on special education.

The key issues before the staffing were whether the child involved should (1) continue to receive speech therapy from Miss Bressler, or (2) receive alternate treatment, or (3) be removed from treatment. It would not be profitable to consider all of the matters examined. But some elements do deserve mention. Care was taken to insure that a complete file was put before the group; when certain documents seemed lacking, an immediate phone call was made to obtain supplementary information. Differences of opinion were frankly examined, and discussed in a serious but professional manner. It gradually became evident that Miss Bressler, the therapist, and the psychologist differed as to the child's rate of progress, and the appropriateness of continuing treatment (which supplemented the child's classroom instruction) (see photo 53).

Mrs. Culverwell, though low key, played an important role in insuring that all alternatives were explored. Eventually a consensus was reached: Miss Bressler would continue treatment, and the case would be reexamined in September. The group then took a break from their cluttered table, before considering their next case.

The mother, who was present, seemed to appreciate the evident concern of all group members with her child's welfare. However, sometimes there are sharp differences between parents and individual group members, or the body of the group. After all, children are sometimes in special education because they are being poorly maintained at home. Furthermore, some parents find it difficult to recognize and admit their child's profound defects. Staffings obviously have a great potential for generating collective irresponsibility, since responsibility is so diffused.

53

Later that day, Mrs. Culverwell invited me to examine the file involved in the staffing. I saw that the diverse evaluations produced recommendations that would be reflected in Miss Bressler's further treatment of the child. In other words, the "stand pat" decision still generated valuable intellectual outcomes.

The school has between thirty and fifty full staffings a year, plus a number of periodic reviews. Obviously, such activities absorb a considerable amount of professional energy.

THE PTA MEETING

At 8:30, on Thursday, January 7, I attended a meeting of the governing board of the school PTA, on the stage of the empty auditorium. One important topic considered was the PTA's annual awards to particular Reilly teachers. The awards would be largely symbolic, but the public announcement would be supplemented with small presents, purchased from the limited treasury. The board was comprised of four members (all mothers) plus, as an advisory member, Mrs. DePaul, the school's math consultant.

One teacher, Mrs. Z, had clearly not been in sympathy with the strike. She had even crossed the picket line (at the district office), and thus reported to work during the strike. Several board members mused as to whether that teacher should be one of the awardees—because of the dedication she had shown by her conduct. Mrs. Kane, the PTA president, remarked, "I know that many of the teachers do not have a great love for Mrs. Z, but she did cross the picket line. In fact, I have even thanked her for that."

Mrs. DePaul mused that the teacher involved was at odds with other faculty members for many reasons—not merely her strike conduct (and I know this to be the case). She suggested it would be poor policy for the board to further aggravate a continuing conflict. Another board member mentioned that the award would be settled by a board vote, and that Mrs. DePaul would not be present.

On Friday, January 8, I ran across a group photograph in the taking. Miss Moffat, with a combined third/fourth grade class, was chair of the committee to order stencilled "tee" shirts and other such materials for the school. They were sold to students, parents, and teachers, to heighten school spirit and raise funds for special projects. She had the idea of providing all members of her class with special shirts, with the class's designation and all the students' names stencilled on. She bought such shirts from her own funds, and they had recently arrived. The pupils, Miss Moffat, and Mrs. Culverwell, wearing the new shirts, posed for a group picture. Mrs. Barreto, Mrs. Lucas' aide, acted as photographer (see photo 54).

On Monday, January 11, before nine, I attended the last part of the meeting of the Discipline Committee. The chair, Mrs. Talbert, was a special education teacher. The committee members seemed informed about their particular charges, and cross-checked each other's insights. The discussion was realistic and engaged. I heard remarks (about different pupils) such as,

"He's just come back from four weeks in Mexico."
"When his mother comes in, she's always reeking with alcohol."
"He just won't do work for Miss Nicks."
"He's accepting of male figures in the school."

When classes began, I went to Mrs. Windham's room.

55

She had again moved her desk, to another side of the class. She was obviously experimenting to decide what spot gave her the optimum control. Shortly after the class began, she took one reading group of twenty-three pupils to the side, and began working with them (see photo 55). (She later mentioned to me that she was considering the merits of starting a third reading group.) Meanwhile, the other students—in a second group—were engaged in seatwork.

SOME HISTORY

On Tuesday, January 12, I visited the school with a university colleague who specializes in urban history. He pointed out some of the unique characteristics of the nearly seventy-five year old Reilly building. The building's designers had not been reluctant to spend extra money to give it an impressive appearance (see photo 56). Cornices, crosshatched bricking, and corbels were all applied for such purposes. Furthermore, the vestibule had been designed to use eight foot high glass doors; those doors had been replaced by wooden panelling, and three-by-six wooden doors. The school's auditorium was large and surely costly.

My colleague's point was that citizens and administrators in the early twentieth century believed that public schools should be "palaces of learning." All of these expenses occurred in an era that was relatively poorer than our time. In a later conversation with Mrs. Culverwell, she agreed that more recently constructed Chicago public schools were designed with greater emphasis on utilitarian economy.

Before the start of school on January 13, I dropped into the teachers' lounge. Mrs. Estes half-jokingly thanking some

teachers for their prayers—she had just received favorable news about a physical exam she had undergone for internal pains. I know her gratitude was not trivial. She had earlier mentioned her fear about the pains, and the forthcoming exam.

In the library at about 8:35, two separate committee meetings were underway in different parts of the room. Mrs. Culverwell flitted between each. One was the Safety Committee. She asked the committee members where the building engineer (Ralph's replacement) was; his presence was appropriate to their business. She said, "As a matter of fact, I mentioned this meeting to him yesterday, and asked he be sure to attend."

Mrs. Culverwell switched on the school intercom—a

56

57

mike and speaker for the intercom was contained in every working room in the building. She asked Mrs. Greenwald, the secretary in the office, to locate the engineer, and send him to the meeting. She said "Remind him that I told him of this meeting yesterday." Her remarks were audible to the ten or so persons throughout the library. The message came back that the engineer was out of the building on an errand. Dom Colagrossi, the assistant engineer, came up instead. He was apologetic, though the committee members realized it was not his fault. To me, the incident was a typical demonstration of Mrs. Culverwell's willingness to rely on public confrontation as one means of asserting authority. Anyone witnessing the episode would surely be reluctant to disregard Mrs. Culverwell's directions in the future; they, too, might risk triggering an equivalent response.

Later in the morning, I rendered a small service. Mrs. Rodriguez had asked me to take a group shot of the Reilly Bilingual Twirlers, a special activity she sponsored for girls in the Spanish program (she herself had been on a championship twirling team in her schooldays). They assembled in the library for their photo shortly before classes began (see photo 57).

IN CLASSROOMS

I then visited Mrs. Lucas' class. I heard Mrs. Gilmore, an aide, explaining to Mrs. Lucas and Mrs. Barreto that she noticed that one of Mrs. Lucas' girl pupils was often poorly dressed. Mrs. Gilmore had some extra little girl's clothes.

58

She asked if Mrs. Barreto could write a note in Spanish to the child's mother, asking her if she would mind receiving the extra clothes as a gift. Mrs. Lucas said the proposal was lovely. Mrs. Barreto promptly sat down to write the note.

Later, I asked Mrs. Lucas' impressions about the progress of her class, and the challenges it involved. She emphasized the simultaneous need for planning and flexibility. It was hard for her pupils to persevere. For them, fifteen minutes was a long time. Their rates of learning are also quite unpredictable. She must have a variety of activities and methods available, and keep many factors in her mind at once. I asked her how she felt about teaching, and why she persisted in such obviously arduous work. She said, "It sounds like a cliche, but I get a great satisfaction from sharing myself. When a child's face lights up with discovery, I feel I can keep teaching forever. When you teach a small class like this, you can get heavily involved. You can have intimacy. It's like a family."

A day or two later, I took a photo of Mrs. Lucas engaged in getting something across to Abraham—one of her more difficult students. The photo expresses the spirit of her remarks (see photo 58).

As I entered the school on Friday, January 15, I saw several members of the Student Council updating the names on the bulletin boards in the vestibule (see photo 59). The

59

60

boards were captioned "Citizenship," "Budding Scholars,"
and "Honor Roll." Other boards listed the names of council
members, and students in other significant activities. The
boards, in the most prominent site in the school, were
simply another instance of the school's deliberate exploitation of its walls to shape the school's environment. It
reminded me that one of the better ways to judge a school's
quality is to examine what it has posted immediately inside
its main door. Reilly's vestibule is covered with announcements honoring the activities of individual pupils and
groups of pupils. It was also no coincidence that the names
were posted by council members. The adults assumed that
council members, as well as the school's faculty, shared an
interest in honoring deserving pupils.

I noticed that upper grade pupils were not listed on the
Honor Roll, but only as Budding Scholars—the category
below Honor Roll. I later asked Mrs. Culverwell about this
pattern. She said the upper grade teachers applied tougher
grading, to prepare pupils for the rigors of high school. She
added that a standard that keeps all upper graders off the
Honor Roll might be too high, and our discussion ended
there. (Later, at the end of the school year, there was further
reference to this possible anomaly.)

On the morning of Friday, January 15, I visited Mrs.

Canepa's room. While class was in progress, Miss Nicks
came to the door. After briefly chatting with Mrs. Canepa,
she went to a girl student, and asked her to leave the classroom with her. I followed. They walked down the hall and
engaged in a brief, apparently serious, conversation (see
photo 60). They then both returned to their previous activities. Later, I asked Miss Nicks what happened. She said
another girl had told her that Mrs. Canepa's student had
threatened to "get her" via fighting after school. Miss Nicks
had confronted the accused student. She felt her intervention had insured that no fight (or other retaliation) would occur.

On Tuesday, January 19, I asked Ms. Humphery about
teaching, and the progress of the year. She said she had been
teaching for fourteen years, and that it has kept her young.
She likes working with children. "They're lumps of clay you
can help to mold," she said. There had been many trans-
fers-in—six students so far this year—but those things happen. "I like teaching, because I can be my own boss."

Since she's a forceful person, I asked her about her interest in administration. "Administration takes too much
manipulation; that's not my style." She especially liked
teaching math. She has favored departmental arrangements
in the school—such as the ones she has helped to develop.

She now teaches advanced math at Reilly to a mixture of students from several classes. The many pull-out activities in the school—bilingual, Student Council, special ed help, Great Books—sometimes make organization frustrating. But it is possible to get along, Ms. Humphery says, if you keep thinking about the good of the children.

During the morning of Wednesday, January 20, I visited Mrs. Canepa's room. She was preparing to briefly leave the class and was describing, to an aide who would hold the fort, what assignments were underway. I later found what her exit was about: one of her homeroom pupils had consistently acted disrespectfully towards some teachers, though he had gotten along well with Mrs. Canepa. His mother had been asked to come to school for a discipline conference, and Mrs. Canepa was expected to participate.

I did not notice many discipline problems in my visits, but the school maintained fairly rigorous standards. It suppressed potential disorder before it went too far. In addition, pupils were rarely left unsupervised long enough for serious trouble to begin. There were only a few "weak" teachers who could not maintain effective discipline, none of whom were among my five regular visitees. (One reason for their exclusion was that they would be too uncomfortable with routine observation.) Two of the three teachers harassed by Mrs. Canepa's pupil were among the school's less effective teachers. But the competent teachers—the preponderant group—realized they had to support teachers who could be targets for disorderly pupils.

I later asked Mrs. Canepa her estimate of the effect of the conference. She was not too sanguine. "For all I can tell, the mother may be more scared of her son than he is of her."

When I went to Ms. Humphery's class, a science lesson was beginning. She demonstrated to the pupils how different objects—including lengths of string—could be vibrated to generate sound waves. Ms. Humphery then initiated a contest, where each student would design a different vibration system to create a sound, and bring it into class. The challenge caught their interest.

BOREDOM

I returned to Mrs. Canepa's class and was reminded of a less satisfying pedagogical matter: pupil boredom. Mrs. Canepa and I had several discussions about the evidently low levels of interest affecting some pupils in her classes. There was little intrusive disorder; she was too able a disciplinarian to permit that, and the pupils involved were not conspicuously aggressive. Furthermore, the patterns of indifference rarely affected a majority of any particular class—though some of her four classes had higher levels thar others.

From visiting some of these same classes when they were with other seventh and eighth grade teachers, it seemed the disaffection was higher in Mrs. Canepa's class than in some others, but other upper level teachers shared some of her dissatisfaction. And even the differences I observed were not necessarily due to individual teachers as much as they may have been the effects of different subject matters.

Boredom evinced itself in different ways—pupils looking away from class activities; pupils writing notes to others during lectures; and pupils writing on their hands in pen to pass the time. Not all pupils involved were, in Mrs. Canepa's view, weak students—though some surely were.

Probably some other teachers could present the same subject matter more engagingly than Mrs. Canepa sometimes did, but there is a greater variable than this. Many educators have observed that pupil interest in learning declines in higher grades. What I observed in the school was only an instance of this common phenomena. A multiplicity of factors underlie such patterns:

- During adolescence, pupils' ranges of capability widen, and differences among pupils become more substantial, and it is harder for teachers to aim instruction towards a relatively divergent group.
- As pupils mature, many see decreasing relevance between parts of their curriculum and their emerging interests; most pupils can see some relevance in learning a little about the characteristics of sound; however, as subjects become more esoteric, more pupils feel like turning away.

Mrs. Culverwell told me a story that illustrates the point. One of her five daughters was intelligent and energetic, but not very interested in formal education. Eventually, she realized she wanted to learn about cooking—to become a chef and perhaps even manage a restaurant kitchen. She enrolled in a rigorous and elaborate formal training program in cooking, and is now working hard and doing well in a cooking school. Given the diversity of talents that human beings display, it is not surprising that many children entering adolescence feel there is a poor match between the school's academic subjects and their potential adult aspirations.

It is also normal and healthy for many maturing pupils to "test" their environments, to see whether they can or should satisfy the demands that institutions place on them. But many of the learning experiences provided for upper grade pupils involve the same tests as the experiences set before first graders. This uniformity does not facilitate sound maturation. It is therefore not surprising that many pupils intellectually withdraw.

Junior high schools were "invented" to provide younger adolescents with appropriate maturing experiences, supposedly designed especially for them. But there is no serious data to show that such pupils learn more or do better in high school than pupils in K through eighth grade schools, such as Reilly. It is also notable that there are findings that junior highs are even less developmentally appropriate for early adolescents than elementary schools. At least, in schools like Reilly, older pupils are provided with one novel and significant responsibility—taking care of younger pupils in manifold ways. And it seems the older Reilly pupils regard such responsibilities as rewarding and significant.

FAREWELL

At the school on the next day, I saw a notice beside the teachers' sign-in sheet. It announced a farewell party for Dom Colagrossi, one of the maintenance men. The party was in the teacher lounge during in-school recess that morning.

The party was carefully planned. Cake (with candles) and coffee were served. A presentation text had been drafted by the Social Committee. It was jointly read by Mrs. Fotos and Mrs. DePaul, the co-chairs. It recited Dom's contributions to the school, including his two years' sponsorship of the school basketball team. Dom—a big, warm guy—seemed almost teary. The gifts included a framed plaque containing a photo of the basketball team, a bottle of Rob Roy scotch, a gift certificate from a prestigious department store, the good wishes card signed by all faculty, and—as Mrs. Canepa's joke—a six-pack of beer (see photo 61). (Earlier in the day, I had noticed two of Mrs. Canepa's pupils, scurrying through the school, collecting the signatures for Dom—whom they evidently knew well.)

As the affair broke up, Miss Swiatek congratulated the two presenters on their lavish praise of Dom. She said, "You did it well. Too often, we fail to give people the credit they deserve."

When I arrived at Mrs. Lucas' room, the pupils were eating lunch. A small incident demonstrated her elaborate teaching concerns.

One pupil, Abraham, had helped pick up the lunches for the class. He was thus entitled to a dish generally regarded as a special treat, but Abraham indicated he did not want to eat his treat. Mrs. Lucas remarked that he should then give the treat to another of the lunch helpers, rather than holding on to it and then throwing it away (see photo 62). Such instruction in "basic manners" was a critical part of her work. For a while, Abraham sulked over his dish—he wanted to

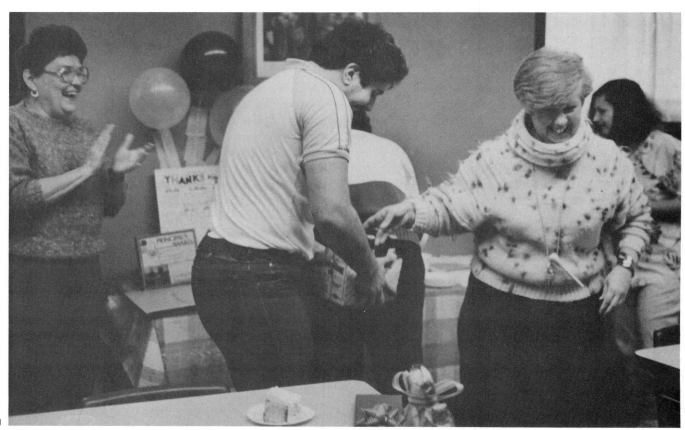

61

63

possess it, but not eat it. Eventually, however, he got up from his desk and took the treat to the other pupil. Mrs. Lucas praised Abraham, made sure the treat recipient thanked him, and resumed her lunch.

In Mrs. Windham's room, a lesson was underway which engaged all the pupils' interest (see photo 63). Each table was supplied with several large globes. Students were provided with instructions, and also quizzed on their ability to locate particular sites on their globes. They were also invited to show each other some of the remote areas where they or their parents came from.

At school at about eight in the morning, on Monday, January 25, I ran across Miss Nicks and Mrs. Ebner, two upper grade teachers, in the front office. They were meeting with a mother and her son to discuss the boy's discipline problems. The meeting must have been embarrassing for both the mother and the boy—the critical tenor of their remarks was evident to the various persons passing through the semi-public office.

A basic Reilly tactic in cases of persisting pupil disorder—and poor parental cooperation—is to create situations where such public criticism occurs. The public situation is partly a by-product of the school's lack of privacy; there is little space where private discussions can easily occur. But beyond this, many of the teachers also believe in "shame" as one alternative discipline technique. Parents should be shamed if they do not show responsibility towards their children. Such shaming stimulates the parents to reassert

control, and display responsibility. Oftentimes, public criticism of pupils is partly motivated by the desire to generate shame as well, for significant disobedience.

In the process of shaming parents, considerable parent aggravation is generated towards the teachers who engage in the "shaming," and sometimes towards the recalcitrant child. However, the teachers do not believe their first responsibility is to win love, but to help children, and they usually only try shaming in desperate situations. Putting it directly, the teachers essentially feel it is more important that the parents fear and respect the school than that they fear their own children.

COMPLAINTS ARISE

The next morning, before classes began, I sat in on a regular meeting of the intermediate grade teachers. It included a purposeful, but good humored discussion of the many schoolwide activities that had recently been completed, or were scheduled for the near future. The teachers were concerned about conflicting priorities in the school (see photo 64). Before the meeting ended, the PA announced a meeting of the school's Professional Problems Committee, starting at once in Mrs. Culverwell's office. The committee formally represents the staff's interest as union members, especially monitoring to see that the union contract is complied with. The PPC is comprised of Mrs. Gibson, the elected union delegate from the school, and designated staff members.

I immediately went to the PPC meeting. It set about discussing a variety of items on an agenda that had been previously delivered to Mrs. Culverwell. The meeting's tone was serious and respectful. Essentially, it picked up some of the themes from the intermediate grade meeting: the school was trying to do too many things at once; the teachers felt harried.

Mrs. Culverwell listened patiently, and occasionally pressed for specifics. The shared concerns among the people involved were impressive. There were no villains—simply professionals with conflicting important priorities. After about ten minutes, it began to seem that the meeting would probably run over until the next day, since classes would begin in a few minutes. But at about one minute to nine, Mrs. Culverwell briefly excused herself, walked to her door, and called over Mrs. Greenwald, the secretary.

She asked her to have the classes of the committee members briefly covered (so the meeting could be carried through to conclusion). She designated the aides and staff members to be assigned that task. Mrs. Culverwell returned to the meeting and it continued. All of the committee

members heard her directions to the secretary. I stayed for part of the remainder of the meeting. It seemed evident that people were working towards a satisfactory compromise solution, where they identified some corrective steps that could be immediately taken.

I found the whole episode very impressive. In a later discussion, I congratulated Mrs. Culverwell on her handling of the situation. She might have used the beginning of classes as an excuse to run from a potential confrontation. Instead, she has proven her right to leadership by demonstrating good faith, vital authority, and an interest in team play. In a way, she "won" the meeting by striving to let it continue, instead of using a legitimate excuse to run away.

I later told this incident to a friend familiar with Chicago school policies. To him, the most striking thing was the school had the "extra" staff available to permit such a quick shift of assignments. I attribute such availability to several factors—because of a strong team spirit, Reilly staff are willing to take on work that goes above and beyond their job descriptions; Mrs. Culverwell tactfully but aggressively pushed for all the staff to which the school was entitled; and many people in the board office respected the school's general efficacy, and were disposed to cooperate with its requests for help.

64

DISORDER

On the morning of Friday, February 5, I visited Mrs. Windham's class. She was getting ready to leave for a break, while her class was handled by a Mrs. Z, a teacher who presented certain special subjects. As Mrs. Z came in, and Mrs. Windham left, I detected special enthusiasm among the pupils. The cause for the ripple soon became evident. The usually well-behaved pupils treated the class as a chance for a lark. Mrs. Z's presentation was lackluster, and she had little ability to maintain discipline. The students had obviously anticipated such mismanagement, and looked forward to taking advantage of it. This was the only poorly disciplined class period I had seen so far in Reilly.

A few of the girls in the class—the most conscientious students—tried to treat the teacher's lecture and questions seriously, but most pupils ignored the presentation and focused on personal and social concerns. The teacher isolated several disorderly pupils at the side of the room. But these pupils then engaged in disruptive by-play with each other.

The episode reminded me of a conversation with Ms. Humphery. She had emphasized that a key test of a teacher's disciplinary ability was the conduct of the class when it was managed by someone else, such as a substitute teacher. Can the regular teacher maintain discipline via a proxy? It was not surprising that Mrs. Windham, the least experienced of my teachers, experienced difficulty in this matter.

I later mentioned my observations to Mrs. Culverwell. She did not question their accuracy. She was familiar with this tenured teacher's deficiencies.

Any large, relatively long-persisting institution eventually will collect a certain proportion of deadwood. Two general—and overlapping—principles can be applied to constructively deal with this inevitable danger: (1) institutions can be extraordinarily careful about who they hire, admit, or enroll, and can have lengthy and thorough screenings and on-the-job probations; and (2) many safeguards and incentives can be established to encourage and pressure less competent employees to leave, and to encourage top managers to weed such persons out.

Public schools, in general, apply insufficient attention to the problem of keeping out or culling deadwood. This is due to a variety of factors, which cannot be outlined in detail here. But one element of the Chicago situation is enlightening, and typical of the constraints that apply in many public school situations. Under the procedures applicable at the time of my visit, a teacher discharged for incompetency must have had his/her work evaluated as "unsatisfactory" by the district superintendent, after one or more classroom visits—as well as innumerable visits by the teacher's princi-

pal. Mrs. Figueroa, Mrs. Culverwell's superintendent, manages twenty-three separate schools, with about 1,000 teachers. The demands on her time are obviously immense. Furthermore, in any particular visit, an incompetent teacher may do an adequate or at least marginal job. And so the superintendent may have to visit the class of an allegedly incompetent teacher several times to establish a case.

Extensive job security "safeguards" apply to tenured teachers in most school systems. Discharge of a tenured teacher is a realistic alternative in only the most egregious situations. I just can't say whether it would be wise for Mrs. Culverwell to dedicate herself to trying to discharge her school's (to my knowledge) two really unsatisfactory tenured teachers, whom she had inherited via diverse circumstances. She might have lost her "case," and I have no idea how vigorously the District Superintendent would support her. I can say that no hospital would have kept people with comparable deficiencies as nurses, no supermarket would have kept them as checkout clerks, and no garage would have kept them as mechanics.

A former president of the Chicago School Board summed up the matter as follows:

> When I took office, I asked how many persons had been discharged in the last year for incompetency. After all, there are over 20,000 employees. I was told there were no such discharges. It was mentioned that there were a certain number of discharges for drunkenness, pilfering, and other semi-criminal acts. Presumably, as long as a person did not violate the law, he was competent. I do not believe that is a sound definition.

IN CLASSROOMS

On Monday, February 8, I attended a meeting of the Discipline Committee. Mrs. Talbert, the chair, excited attention by announcing that she was transferring out of Reilly. Each day, her drive to the school was thirty miles in one direction. Another well-reputed Chicago public school, much nearer her home, had a vacancy and had accepted Mrs. Talbert's application. The other staff at the meeting expressed their best wishes and regrets.

The next day, in the early afternoon, I saw the effects of a reorganization in Ms. Humphery's class—though it had been occurring for some time in my absence. An advanced math class, taught by Ms. Humphery, had been carved out of two separate classes, after considerable planning. The class pooled the more able math students. These students were brought together daily at a determined time in Ms. Humphery's room. Meanwhile, the less adept students

65

were grouped in Mrs. Foto's room for their focused instruction.

Naturally such measures took planning and good pupil discipline, so little time would be lost in the shifts. In the photo, Ms. Humphery is scanning her text and lesson plan for the approaching session (see photo 65).

Later in the day, I dropped by a meeting of the Student Council, moderated by Miss Nicks. The council, with her leadership, was planning the last details for the school's Valentine Dance. Towards the end of the discussion, Miss Nicks mentioned that, since the primary grades would be left out of the dance, the council would conduct some special activity for those grades at Easter; some reference was made to visits by the Easter Bunny. She also mentioned that any income from the dance would be used for that purpose.

The school celebrated Valentine's Day on Thursday, February 11. When I arrived at noon, I quickly got some sense of the occasion. A mother, in the vestibule, was priming her preschool children for their in-class Valentine's party. Other elements of the occasion soon became evident. In Mrs. Windham's room, a mother-volunteer had come to class, to help with activities wearing her own elaborate nineteenth century style gown, which she used for party purposes. She also mentioned to me that the gown style was in keeping with the theme of Lincoln's Birthday. Mrs. Windham's pupils received Valentine cards and opened them

67

with great enthusiasm, accompanied by treats of cookies and pop (see photo 66).

While the festivities continued, school life also went on. Mrs. Culverwell met and interviewed Mrs. Hinggbotham, an applicant for Mrs. Talbert's job. Mrs. Hinggbotham was an experienced Chicago teacher. Her family had been out of the state for several years, and had recently moved back into the city. She was trying to resume employment with the board, and had been referred to the school by the board. Mrs. Culverwell was impressed with her experience and energy, and took her for a tour of the school—to help "sell" her on the job, and further size her up. During the tour, they ran across two teachers, Miss Moffat and Ms. Landes. It seems Mrs. Hinggbotham and Ms. Landes had formerly worked together in another school. Ms. Landes vigorously encouraged her to come to work at Reilly (see photo 67).

Chapter Six

GRANTING AWARDS

Dear Parent:

We are alerting you that there has been a case of head lice in Room _____. This can pass from person to person through close physical contact or through the use of personal articles such as clothing, combs, brushes, towels, and bedding. The head louse is found in the hair; and its eggs (nits), as small grayish objects attached to the individual hairs. The nits are usually found behind the ears.

(Extract from a form letter to parents kept available in school files.)

THE school holds two "awards assemblies" each year. These ceremonies honor students who have shown different forms of exemplary performance. One awards assembly was scheduled for the middle of March. Before examining this honoring process, I decided I would have to see more of the routine life of the school; the seeds of honor are planted in mundane matters.

IN CLASSROOMS

After classes began on Monday, February 15, I visited Ms. Humphery. During a brief break, with a wry smile she showed me an absence excuse note just received from a parent. The mother asked that her daughter be excused, since she had to stay home and catch up on her sleep. Over the weekend she had attended a friend's birthday party, and been "pressured" by her peers to stay at the party until 4 A.M. The note concluded with the remark, "Kids are so mean these days." Naturally, both Ms. Humphery and I shared our wonderment at a mother who would leave a ten year old unaccounted for until 4 A.M.

Next I sat in on Mrs. Canepa's class, during Mrs. Culverwell's evaluation visit. The lesson presented was on planning written or oral arguments, such as debates. In particu-

lar, Mrs. Canepa asked her pupils to raise their hands, and propose pro and con arguments about the comparative merits of dogs and cats as pets. Those arguments would provide the framework for a hypothetical debate presentation. The topic generated unusual interest. The students listened intently, and volunteered many ingenious arguments. Mrs. Canepa listed the arguments on the board, and then divided them into discrete categories. She presented the material with her usual brio. (As an interesting aside, it was significant to discover that about half the pupils in the class did not know the meaning of "capital punishment." The words came up during the class discussion, and a simple survey was then conducted. I do not know what one should expect from twelve year olds, but it is useful to be reminded of some of their limits.)

The students involved—from Mrs. Canepa's homeroom—showed more enthusiasm than usual (see photo 68). Were they trying to make their likeable teacher look good in front of the principal, since they surely observed Mrs. Culverwell's presence? Or was it simply that the topic was inherently appealing—it tapped their common current knowledge levels, required no studying, and enabled everyone to contribute something? I also wondered about the wisdom of letting each teacher choose the occasion for their visitation; Mrs. Canepa could probably foretell that this topic would be far more interesting to her pupils than some other prescribed lessons. But Mrs. Culverwell had many other sources of information about Mrs. Canepa's abilities and challenges, and I am confident that no serious deception occurred.

After the class was dismissed, Mrs. Culverwell handed Mrs. Canepa a copy of her handwritten evaluation, and they discussed Mrs. Culverwell's reactions, which were understandably favorable. A more deliberate discussion was scheduled for the near future.

FOUNDER'S DAY

Thursday was the PTA's annual Founder's Day celebration. It was also their celebration of the 200th anniversary of the United States Constitution. The occasion was held in the

68

library. Six former presidents of the chapter (the "founders") attended. They each were introduced and said a few words. Two visitors from the American Legion were present; one of them delivered an address on the significance of the Constitution to the twenty or so PTA members. The photo shows Mr. Corbett, one of the Legionnaires, talking to Mrs. Nelson, a PTA officer (see photo 69). The Kandinsky picture in the background is also relevant—Mrs. Nelson is the Picture Lady for the school. Under a program sponsored by the Chicago Art Institute, she regularly arranges for reproductions of significant pictures to be displayed in the school, along with exploratory texts that are communicated to students. The Kandinsky is one of "her" pictures.

Later the teachers, taking advantage of indoor recess, joined the group and enjoyed a snack prepared by the PTA.

Mrs. Kane then announced that the chapter had attained 100 percent membership among the school's parents (largely due, as all knew, to her determination). In gratitude for the teachers' help in attaining that success, the chapter contributed two VCR players to the school, for use in presenting video teaching materials. Mrs. Kane also announced the chapter had designated Miss Swiatek and Mrs. Delgado as the school's teachers of the year. Detailed citations of their achievements were read aloud. Each was provided with a small gift, amidst applause from the gathering.

The PTA's award process represented a healthy division of authority. If necessary, Mrs. Culverwell would have been able to designate the school's one or two teachers of the year—but it would be a vexing process, with a high potential for aggravation. The matter would be especially touchy because the criteria would necessarily be ambiguous. It certainly involved more than simply identifying the teacher with the best attendance. At the same time, the school was dedicated to recognizing merit wherever it occurred. The PTA was distant enough from the school administration for its conclusions to be seen as independent—and close enough to the school situation to develop an informed and respectable opinion (recall how the PTA was counselled away, for diverse reasons, from designating the strikebreaker as winner).

Later that morning, I attended Mrs. Culverwell's evaluation visit to Mrs. Estes. Mrs. Estes was engaged in teaching her pupils phonics. As I had seen on several occasions, she lined up the pupils at the board, and had them write columns of syllables. She then designated particular students to read the syllables. Mrs. Culverwell sat off to the side, observing the process, and taking notes. Sometimes she got up and walked around, looked over the documents on Mrs. Estes' desk and the work the pupils did.

One item on the blackboard deserves particular comment. There was a chalked-in running tabulation of the boys' and girls' contributions to the school's Crusade of Mercy (the local community chest) drive. Also each student has his or her name and contribution listed separately. The contributions ran from $.31 to $5.00. Most other classrooms listed boy and girl tabulations for the drive, though I do not know if any also listed individual pupil names.

Undoubtedly, some adults might question the wisdom of applying such "pressure" tactics to young children, especially when the community was not especially wealthy. But I believe I know Mrs. Estes' "case" for that practice, from what I have observed in her class. She presumes that everybody is capable of giving something, since being a giver is one aspect of human dignity. Furthermore, she—and indeed the whole school—believes that we do and should judge each others' conduct. One object of such judging is the process of public contribution. There can be no vital system of public praise—and the school strongly believes in such praise—without the possibility of public rebuke. As the adult in charge, she believes that she can manage the collection process so that no severe tensions occur.

IN THE LOUNGE

On Monday, February 22, in the teachers' lounge before classes, I saw an interesting instance of teacher disapproval. Mrs. Z, one of the weak teachers, happened to be sitting in the lounge, with others sitting or standing around. The teacher remarked, "I'm not too happy; my evaluation visit is

69

70

coming up." The words were obviously uttered to stimulate a sympathetic response. If I heard them, surely the others did too. I was surprised that not one of the usually supportive teachers uttered a word of comment. The remark just dropped flat in the room, and the conversation drifted to other things.

I then went down to the main doors, to observe the first-day-of-the-week entry of pupils. In Ms. Humphery's room, it was interesting to observe the speed and discipline of the pupils' start: at 9:07, after flag salute and lunch money collection, they were hard at work (see photo 70).

In Mrs. Canepa's class, things were more complicated. The students were assigned to present oral recitations. When they were individually called on, a high proportion of them were not prepared, despite adequate advance notice. While early adolescents might be interested in listing the pros and cons of cats and dogs, they are much less disposed to memorize and present a brief formal statement of some position. It was intriguing that James Johnson, one of the often reluctant pupils, came in prepared, and delivered a properly memorized and articulated poem (see photo 71). At the conclusion, he mentioned that it had been written by his mother. Mrs. Canepa offered her congratulations on both the poem and his delivery. She said, in a loud tone, "James

Johnson, 96 percent; Linda Johnson, 100 percent." The opening stanza of the poem follows:

> *Everyone in this world,*
> *Can have a dream or two,*
> *But only in America,*
> *Can you make those dreams come true.*

There was a half-hour in-service on February 23. Mrs. Culverwell was out with a nagging virus, and Miss Swiatek presided. One of the meeting's major themes was getting 100 percent teacher participation in the Crusade of Mercy. Miss Swiatek was the chair of the school drive, and made the basic "pitch." I knew some of teachers were cool to the matter, and resented the board's vigorous urgings for contributions. Miss Swiatek stepped up to the podium and delivered a clear and forceful presentation. It may not have persuaded all the objectors, but it made a good case. After the meeting, one of the teachers said to me, in an equivocal manner, "That Jayne (Swiatek), isn't she something!" I responded in kind, "Well, given her job, she sure better be."

On February 24, I watched Mrs. Windham lead her class in their practice for the music assembly (see photo 72). Many of her pupils, incidentally, were wearing their Reilly

71

72

tee shirts, which had recently been delivered. In Mrs. Estes' room, the story of the day on the blackboard also pointed up the theme of the coming assembly: "Today is Wednesday. Don't forget the assembly on Friday. Be sure to look your best."

In Mrs. Canepa's class, the oral recitations were still continuing. While all students were eventually required to recite, she had turned from drafting reciters to first calling on volunteers.

Mrs. Lucas and Mrs. Barreto were leading their children through a series of simple games. Such activities were especially important for their class; the children usually were not organized enough to engage in deliberate games on their own. In the schoolyard during recess they simply hung around, and were not able to play the games the other pupils started. The photo shows pupils passing under the bridge in "London Bridge" (see photo 73). Mrs. Barreto's participation as part of the bridge is undoubtedly one reason the game went so well.

A CONFRONTATION

At the end of the day, in Mrs. Windham's room, I witnessed a small confrontation. I sensed the class had been somewhat unruly over the past several days. At dismissal time, the matter reached a tacit boiling point. Usually, after

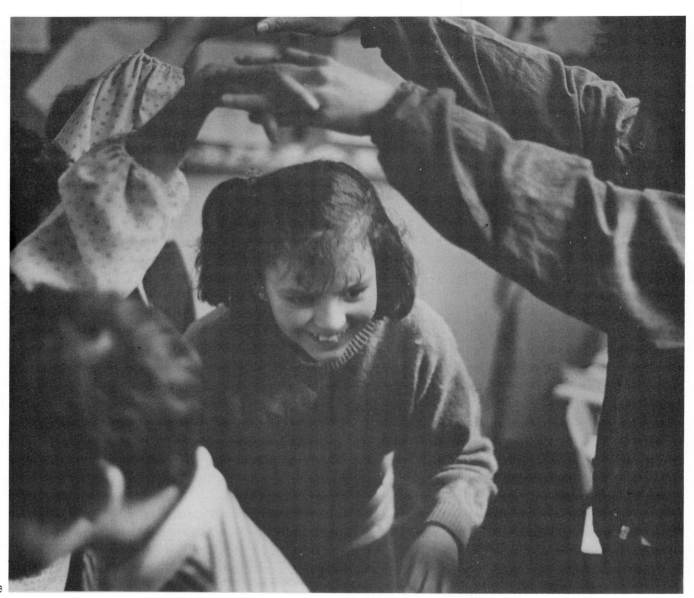

73

74

the students had jackets on, she designated, in succession, the most orderly tables, to put their chairs on their table and get in the dismissal line. But none of the tables were acting orderly enough to justify designation. Even after the chairs were put on the tables, the pupils still continued to wiggle restlessly. Mrs. Windham expressed her displeasure.

She told all the pupils to replace their chairs on the floor, be seated, and wait, even after the dismissal bell rang. Despite this sanction, mild disorder persisted (see photo 74). Several of the more obedient girls expressed their discomfort by going over and hugging their popular teacher, since they were so upset at her annoyance. When Mrs. Windham passed near me in the room, I made a quiet joke to her about the desirability of reestablishing concentration camps; she, with a mixture of a grimace and a smile, nodded in assent. I had to leave the class at 2:35, while most students were still restlessly seated at their tables.

The next day, I discovered Mrs. Windham had spontaneously postponed her car pool for twenty minutes, and held the class until they settled down. I suspect this extreme measure helped convince the students that despite her low key approach, she would draw and hold the line where necessary. From other discussions with Mrs. Windham, I knew she was frustrated by some of her problems in maintaining discipline. Thus, earlier in the school year, she had tried to get parent cooperation by sending notes to the parents of unruly children, but had not had great success. She then resumed her earlier tactic of calling such parents at home in the evening. This was more effective but added to her phone bill.

It was not surprising that Mrs. Windham, the least experienced of my five teachers, had the greatest problems with discipline. This is a common pattern with beginning teachers. It seemed to me that she had trouble reconciling her affection for the pupils with their (sometimes) evident need for fast, stern reprimands. Given her dedication and persistence, I am sure that, in time, she will master that complex act.

On Thursday, February 25, I dropped by Ms. Humphery's room before the beginning of classes. She was meeting with Mrs. Kane, the PTA president, to discuss the progress of one of Mrs. Kane's daughters in her class. The discussion was animated, and the meeting even continued after the student entrance bell — and so Ms. Humphery's students lined up outside the closed door and waited for her to admit them. When the Pledge was recited over the loudspeaker, the

75

whole class—removed from Ms. Humphery's observation—stood at attention, hands on their hearts, and recited it. A moment later, Ms. Humphery ended her conference, walked to the door, and admitted the students.

The episode helped me appreciate a remark Mrs. Culverwell had made at the beginning of the year, when she had termed Ms. Humphery her best disciplinarian. I also recalled that Ms. Humphery had told me one of her prime goals was to educate her students to do the right thing even when she was not present. I had witnessed a final exam.

Later in the morning, I had an interesting chat with Mrs. Kane, the very involved PTA president. She observed that she had dropped out of college to get married, and had not led an organized youth. Now she was engaged in rearing a large family, but still wanted to keep her mind active. She said, "My work around the school stimulates my brain." It was evident that Mrs. Kane, though she did not have a formal role in the school organization, made an important contribution. Indeed, Mrs. Kane may have been even more important because she was not paid. As a volunteer, she would be little inclined to continue in a job unless she was doing something worthwhile; paid employees, in contrast, may despise their work, sometimes with good cause, and still keep at it.

In Mrs. Culverwell's office, I listened to a long conversation between the principal and Mrs. DePaul. It largely focused on the school's reading score patterns. Mrs. DePaul generally oversees the analysis of data from the school's testing program, and also provides Mrs. Culverwell with the data to monitor individual teachers. The two were discussing a teacher whose students were lagging considerably behind in test results. Mrs. Culverwell asked Mrs. DePaul to monitor her teaching, and urge her to improve the pacing of her instruction. The whole discussion was thoughtful and informed. It is notorious that many schools and principals do not make careful use of pupils' test scores to monitor and improve a teacher's performance.

The school's music assemblies were scheduled for Friday, February 26. The photos for both assemblies—the primary (K–5), and upper grade (6–8)—disclose the school's continuing commitment to spectacle and presentation. There was an elaborate posting of the Colors. Carefully rehearsed musical numbers, performed by students in big self-made paper hats, were a popular theme (see photo 75). Some Polish students, dressed in regional costumes, presented folk dances (see photo 76). And Jennifer, a Korean girl from Mrs. Windham's class, played an important part as piano accompanist.

76

IN CLASSROOMS

My next visit was on Tuesday, March 1. In Mrs. Lucas' room, a birthday party was in progress for Claudia, one of her students (see photo 77). Many of the students were obviously enjoying themselves, but some of them could not easily participate in an occasion theoretically dedicated to one particular student.

The library is just beside Mrs. Lucas' room, and so I dropped in there. Mrs. Estes' class was seated at the table, carrying out an assignment from Miss Knott, the librarian. A moment after my arrival, a visitor appeared—Mrs. Evelyn Sloran, a primary teacher who had retired last year. She had returned to visit her friends (see photo 78). The reunion

was partly enriched by Mrs. Estes' class, since some of the pupils in the library had been Mrs. Sloran's pupils last year. They cheerily called out "Good afternoon, Mrs. Sloran." And she responded in kind.

Shortly afterwards, I had a prearranged meeting in the library with two of Mrs. Canepa's students. They had been assigned to interview me for the *Reilly Reporter*, the school paper, about my research. After they had finished their questions, I asked a question of my own.

"Do you like the Reilly school?"

They both replied "Yes."

I then asked "Why?"

One of the "Why?" replies was especially interesting—"I like it because they help you learn."

77

"How do they do that?"

"They make you work. Before going to Reilly, I went to another school. There, nobody cared if you didn't do your homework. Here, if you don't do your homework, they get mad and yell at you. And so they help you learn."

At the end of the day, I had a brief conversation with Mrs. Culverwell. She told me of her family's historic commitment to Chicago public education. Her grandmother had been a Chicago public school teacher. Her mother and two of her aunts had held similar jobs. Mrs. Culverwell herself, was mildly distressed when she had five daughters, and none of them seemed interested in teaching. But, happily, one daughter, after leaving college and going towards a noneducation career, opted to turn to teaching; she was now teaching her first year in the Chicago public schools.

Mrs. Culverwell also reminisced about the relative rigor that once pervaded Chicago school training and hiring policies. When she determined to enter teaching in the 1940s, the principal of each high school in the Chicago area was allowed to nominate two graduates to the Chicago Teachers College—the major route for employment by the board. When one recalls that some of those high schools had grad-uating classes of 500 and more, it is evident that the previous selection process was relatively demanding. Today, much higher proportions of the population are needed in teaching, and many other attractive career options are open to women.

The next morning, in the office, I ran across the first instance I had seen of Mrs. Culverwell losing her temper. Several people had called the school about rumors of head lice among pupils; such infestations are not uncommon among pupils in many schools, but the lice spread rapidly, and the school or class affected has to quickly warn parents, and take other suppressive measures. The inquirers—including people from the district office—asked what measures had been taken against the infestation. But the school had no information about whether and where the incidents were occurring. No complaints had been made about specific classes. And so the situation was awkward; despite the rumors, the school could not do anything.

The mother who had triggered the "rumors" came to the office this morning. Mrs. Culverwell was very upset that she had never brought her complaints directly to the school, so corrective measures could be taken. Instead, she had gone around complaining to third parties. The photo shows her expressing her indignation to the mother (see photo 79). Later in the morning, it turned out that the mother had asked her husband to call the school and present their complaint, but he had never carried through that charge. The lady realized the unfairness of the situation and offered a sincere apology, and the school set about taking the necessary preventives. The matter evaporated.

THE AWARDS ASSEMBLY

Thursday, March 3, in the early afternoon, I attended the upper grade awards assembly, in which the Student Council played a prominent role. One officer spoke at the podium, and welcomed the students; a second delivered an oral report on the council's current activities; and a third officer introduced the council delegates to the audience. Then each delegate mounted to the stage and handed out the awards to his or her particular class.

The major "awards" distributed were Certificates of Merit, for service to the school or class. Students were designated for such certificates by their teachers. The proportions of students in each class receiving certificates varied. How-

ever, I was not surprised to see that, in both Mrs. Windham's and Ms. Humphery's classes, all—or almost all—students received certificates. It was clear to me that high proportions of their students rendered service, as lunch deliverers, hall monitors, collecting papers or money, and other chores. The designated students in each class were brought as a group to the stage, and then came forward at the call of their names to receive certificates.

The students treated the affair quite seriously. While I saw one student on the stage wearing torn jeans, I saw another student take off her padded jacket and leave it at her seat, before going on the stage—to make a better appearance. When I later ran into two awarded students in the hall, they proudly showed their certificates.

After the awards, Mrs. Culverwell came to the podium. She first congratulated the council and Miss Nicks for the organization of the occasion. She then identified other conspicuously successful students—the students designated on the Citizenship Honor Roll (posted in the vestibule); and the two students who had won in the District Science Fair and had been guests at the citywide luncheon for upper level winners. The Color Guards picked up the Colors and trooped out, and the assembly was dismissed.

On Friday, March 4, Mrs. Estes' class went on a field trip.

79

80

Each class had a minimum of two field trips a year. The nature of the trips were largely up to each teacher's discretion. Hopefully, they would represent an effort to relate the children's in-class learning with events and resources in the world at large. In addition, the trips were an occasion for the teacher and pupils to participate in a learning activity away from the normal school structure. It offered them a chance to discover each other in another environment.

Mrs. Estes had heard of a nature center, in an area on the edge of the city. It had a miniature zoo/museum, and the sponsors also tapped sugar maple trees during the early spring—around the beginning of March. She planned a trip to the center. The trip represented a challenge. Some of the activities were out-of-doors, and the weather might be cold.

There also could be a problem keeping track of children at such a location, so she made careful arrangements.

The children arrived at school especially warmly clothed. She had them write their names on squares of paper, and pinned each pupil with a name tag. A parent had been recruited as an additional aide. Right after the beginning of school, they marched out to the bus and took off. During the ride, the pupils were lively, but good humored. The visit to the center was interesting, and the children saw the process of tapping the trees. They especially enjoyed licking the maple sap on their fingers. The well-organized and relatively ambitious trip was a profitable experience (see photo 80).

In the afternoon on Tuesday, March 8, I visited the class-

81

room of Mrs. Ebner, the upper grade math teacher. Mrs. Ebner was one of the school's many assertive and firm teachers. I thought it would be interesting to see her instructing students.

As I entered, the Math Club was meeting under her leadership. This club consisted of the upper grade pupils who had a special facility and interest in math. Nineteen pupils attended. They were divided into five "teams," and worked from a prealgebra text. Shortly after I entered, Mrs. Ebner, I believe partly due to my visit, changed the subject matter she was presenting. She asked the teams to estimate the proper digits to go on the network of empty squares she chalked on the board. Each team was challenged to work together to identify the formula underlying the squares. A hot competition ensued (see photo 81). My visit made it clear to me that Mrs. Ebner, in addition to her firm discipline, knew how to stimulate students.

Most of the Reilly teachers' on-the-side activities, such as Mrs. Ebner's club, are of course done without extra pay. Those activities that are paid—such as committee responsibilities—are parts of teachers' responsibilities authorized by the union contract; but even many of these activities are by-passed in too many schools.

A CONFRONTATION

On Friday, March 11, in Mrs. Canepa's room, a small drama occurred. Shortly after I entered, she called down a boy for disorder. The particular act of mischief did not catch my eye, but I later found it had been preceded by a series of aggravating incidents. The boy responded to the criticism in a sullen fashion. Mrs. Canepa reacted forcefully.

She walked over to his desk, and had him get up and promptly precede her into the hall outside the classroom. There, the two of them confronted each other with the room door open. It is possible that Mrs. Canepa stayed just outside the room with the door open to keep an eye on the class. However, I believe she also intended the class overhear the scene—to warn them of the consequences misconduct could generate, and to heighten the humiliation of the miscreant.

In a clear, loud, and very firm voice, she said, "Do you think I want to take my paycheck from the city while you sit around doing nothing? You may believe that you can call the shots in this school, but you are wrong. At this stage in your life, you are not able to make most of your own decisions. Part of my job is to stop you from ending up as a bum on the streets, even though you don't seem to care much about that danger. . . ."

While the two were in the hall, a certain degree of uneasiness ranged among the students in the unsupervised classroom. I was very impressed at the profound engagement displayed by Mrs. Canepa. It seemed to me to be a form of deep caring. At the end of the reprimand, Mrs. Canepa and the student returned to the room, and she resumed presentation of her regular lesson.

One of my most unexpected discoveries at the school were the virtues of shouting (or voice control) as a vital form of punishment—and how to do it well. A number of the teachers had identified a psychological phenomenon known well to Marine drill instructors: if a person with some authority suddenly yells in someone's face in a belligerent manner at very close range—say about two or three feet—the experience is demoralizing and painful. The "listener" is stressed because he/she does not know how to respond. The close range shouting turns on his/her internal danger signals, but at the same time, he/she is reluctant to attack an obvious superior.

At Reilly, I witnessed both effective and ineffective shouting. Ineffective shouting occurred when it was directed at large, unruly groups, or at students more than three to five feet away. I also believe the effective shouting was used at least with semi-deliberation, as when Mrs. Canepa decided it was time for a showdown. The immediate trigger was a spontaneous situation, but she suspected a confrontation was approaching.

In "successful" shouting situations, the comparative physical sizes of the shouter and listener are not critical. We are all severely reluctant to strike superiors. This is especially so when the aggressive discipline occurs suddenly, without our being psychically prepared. Furthermore, the shouting teachers oftentimes made some gestures to make their criticisms semi-private—such as Mrs. Canepa taking the student outside the classroom. The privacy was imperfect. However, such measures moderated the students' humiliation, and enabled them to save at least some face.

Many Reilly teachers have deliberately perfected this technique. They selectively use it—especially at early stages of the school year—to establish classroom control. Conversely, teachers who had not developed such approaches—such as Mrs. Windham—seemed to spend an inordinate amount of energy devising punishment alternatives, which oftentimes become cumbersome and even counterproductive.

I should also note that none of the effective shouting teachers had trouble being generally warm and supportive towards students. Of the two teachers in the school who were least respected by students, one was a moderately adept shouter who often used her skill for inappropriate ends, and the other was a poor shouter. Both were inadequate disciplinarians; they had no insight into student motivation, and had poor personal self-control.

The entire issue of shouting should also be seen as part of the complex matter of punishment, in general. Punishment is most effective in discouraging bad behavior when it can be administered quickly after violations; is disliked by violators; can be applied in doses of increasing severity; and does not generate great distress for punishers. I am convinced that many schools simply have not devised effective techniques of punishment, and hence there are discipline problems in too many schools. The Reilly shouting system represents one adaptation that satisfies the criteria of effective punishment just outlined.

THE OLYMPICS

On Monday, March 14, I went to another Chicago public elementary school to see Reilly students participate in the system's Academic Olympics. The Olympics take advantage of one feature of the Chicago system that is often a drawback: its large size. That size provides a logical pool for interschool academic competition. Today's Olympics focused on math. A Reilly team had been selected (via an in-class and in-school competition), to compete on behalf of the school. Mrs. Ebner had coached the team.

Each team took a turn on the stage. The members were publicly tested via an oral exam based on questions projected on a screen. The aim was to see which team could achieve the best score (see photo 82). I left before the out-

82

come was determined. The victorious team would advance to the citywide Olympics. The well-organized affair made a very favorable impression on me.

The next day, when I arrived at the school at 8:30, I immediately heard that the math team had made a fine showing. Karen Kane, a daughter of the PTA president, had been the top scorer. I saw several teachers gather to congratulate her.

On Wednesday morning, I dropped by the library to photograph some of the attractive posters (made by pupils) displayed over the bookcases (see photo 83). They were simply another instance of the school's emphasis on shaping its environment.

On the morning of Thursday, March 17, before classes, I

saw a mother bringing her son to the teachers to settle a discipline issue. Miss Nicks had sent several notes home to the mother via her son, but when the notes produced no good effect, the meeting had been arranged. The boy admitted, in his mother's presence, that he had not delivered the notes. He promised to reform, and his mother agreed to monitor his improvement. As the episode was winding up, I noticed that the four math Olympics winners had just been awarded their impressive medals, and were showing them to their teachers. I photographed the medalists as the discipline discussion continued on the other side of the hall (see photo 84).

Before classes began on Monday, March 21, I dropped by the classroom of Mrs. Opehlia Lee. She had eventually been transferred in to replace Mrs. Talbert. I asked her about Mrs. Culverwell's interest and support. She said that it had been helpful and intense; during her first days at the school, Mrs. Culverwell had dropped by for at least brief visits for five days in a row. Mrs. Lee interpreted such visits as a constructive sign. Later, I visited Mrs. Estes' class during lunch. The pupils enjoy eating with each other and their teachers (see photo 85).

When I dropped in on Mrs. Lucas, I found her having a bad day. The students were unusually fractious. While the class was under her control, the students were ill at ease. At one point, she remarked, *sotto voce*, "You guys are the pits." I quietly expressed my sympathies, and left her to her miseries.

85

When I returned to Mrs. Estes' class, this irrepressible woman had gotten her class engaged in making Easter rabbits, from some ingenious combination of styrofoam, cotton, glue, and other materials. Naturally, her students were absorbed by the activity (see photo 86). Oftentimes, she used such art projects as incentives for academic activities; the pupils could work on art after they satisfactorily finished particular academic assignments.

Meanwhile, in the school office, a less gratifying scene was underway. A bussed girl student had brought a long pocketknife (taken from her father's drawer) to school, and then given it to another pupil. Meanwhile, the girl had also cut some seats of the bus with the knife. The student given the knife had reported the matter to a teacher.

Mrs. Culverwell, that very day, called in the child's parents to the school, and reviewed the matter with them in strong terms. She also had the police called immediately to the school, since cutting the seat and bringing the knife into school were crimes. Two plainsclothesmen arrived promptly, met with Mrs. Culverwell, and consulted with the parents and their daughter.

It was Mrs. Culverwell's policy to immediately call the police when a possible criminal act occurred in or around the school. She realized that in many situations the ultimate charges will be dropped, or only a symbolic punishment (e.g., probation) will result. But she believed it was essential to demonstrate that the crimes would be turned over to the police—out of her possibly sympathetic hands. She

86

felt this policy generated strong deterrence, and encouraged pupils to be law abiding. Of course, she also realized police involvement could also injure the school's reputation—criminal acts around the school might be publicized. But the first reputation the school needed was for maintaining the law. Covering up crimes would not aid that reputation.

I know many educators who do not share Mrs. Culverwell's opinion—for example, many schools apply what I believe to be excessive leniency towards various pupil in-school drug violations. Such crimes are not reported to the police even when evidence is available. Allegedly, the educators are "shielding" pupils; all too often, I fear, they are protecting their own reputations.

FUN

When I dropped by Mrs. Estes' class on Wednesday, March 23, she asked if I would be able to hear the class do their music assembly piece, "Kingston Town." I told her I could not make the assembly. She immediately revised the class schedule, and had them perform the song to the accompaniment of different percussion instruments. The children's engagement was notable.

On many occasions, I was struck with the important role "fun" played at Reilly—whether it was in assemblies, daily recess, or in-class activities such as art. Reilly pupils who had been transferred from other public schools reported to me that Reilly had more such "activities" than their previous schools. The activities were not necessarily unstructured, or without content—they might require planning, rehearsals, learning new skills, or considerable efforts by teachers and pupils.

This interweaving of work and play may be especially effective with pupils who come to school from backgrounds not highly supportive of learning. The approach may also be pertinent to the structure of American schools in general. In America, the particular design of formal education keeps unusually high proportions of students in academic programs for more years than in other countries. In other words, nonelitist education systems may have to use more "goodies" to retain student involvement.

The school's pro-activity philosophy undoubtedly enriched relationships among children and adults. Furthermore, it often vitalized school/home contacts, e.g., pupils brought art projects home to parents, parents came to see pupils perform.

When I visited Mrs. Culverwell before leaving, I observed a small reunion. Mrs. Estes, smiling broadly, came to her office, accompanied by a tall, long haired young man, wearing a black tee shirt, with "A" for anarchy boldly let-

87

tered across the front (see photo 87). She introduced him to Mrs. Culverwell as Charles Charapla—"You remember him—one of my special education students." And, indeed, Mrs. Culverwell remembered Charles, and greeted him warmly.

As she later told me, Mrs. Estes had for a number of years taught a special ed class for older pupils at Reilly. Charles had been one of her students—and his situation had not been good. He'd been the picked-on runt of the class, and made much of his trouble for himself. But now he was no longer a runt, and had turned up at Reilly to say "Hello" to Mrs. Estes. Charles, when asked about his current status, said he was attending the neighborhood public high school, and that "I screwed up one year, but now I have my act together, and will graduate this year." In sum, Charles, despite his "anarchic" shirt, seemed quite purposeful. Mrs. Estes was very pleased with his bearing and return visit.

I later discussed the reunion with Mrs. Estes. She reiterated her pleasure at Charles' improvement—though, as she said, "I could hardly resist the temptation to take a scissors and give him a good haircut." She also reminisced about her arduous years in special education: "I finally had to leave because I just did not have any more to give. Here, in first grade, I can see the beneficial effects of my teaching almost every day."

THE EASTER DRESS

On Thursday, the next day, I again dropped in on Mrs. Estes. We got into a conversation about the difficult home situations of some pupils. She remarked that one primary grade girl had most of her clothes destroyed in an incident

89

90

in her home. The two primary teachers, Mrs. Estes and Mrs. Lange, then chipped in to buy her an Easter dress—partly for the forthcoming school Easter Party (see photo 88).

The following Tuesday, I found Ms. Humphery's class being briefly monitored by a substitute, while she was away on an errand. I noticed one boy standing at the back of the class, his face towards the wall. The sub started to say that the punished boy had served his time—he had been put in the back by Ms. Humphery—and should return to his seat. The boy and the class responded loudly, in one voice, "Oh no! He was told to stand there until *she* let him off." The sub then responded, "Well then I guess I can show no mercy." (It was undoubtedly significant that the boy had been placed in a spot which was visible through the classroom door window. If Ms. Humphery casually walked by, she could check out his obedience.) Later, I asked Ms. Humphery for some details: she said that the boy stood, altogether, for about thirty minutes, until she thought the point had been made.

When I dropped by Mrs. Lucas, I found Mrs. Barreto busily engaged in carrying out a lesson with one part of the class, while Mrs. Lucas worked with the remainder (see photo 89). She seemed very comfortable with her evolving responsibilities. Mrs. Barreto, thanks to her talent and Mrs. Lucas' support had come a long way since starting as an aide at the beginning of the year.

The next day, Thursday, March 31, was the last school day before Easter. Bill Presley, a sturdy eighth grader, had been enlisted as the Easter Bunny. He was suitably made up by some Student Council members and briefed by Miss Nicks. He then visited the primary grades, to deliver treats to them. The primary pupils were dressed in their best, and many of them wore ingenious, school-made "bonnets" (see photos 90 and 91).

Chapter Seven

A DAY IN THE LIFE OF THE PRINCIPAL

The principal provides strong leadership and works to identify clear educational goals for the school.

(Excerpt from document about school excellence circulated at a Reilly in-service.)

TO portray one of Mrs. Culverwell's typical work days, I followed her through her in-school day on March 30. I met her at home before her trip to work.

While chatting in her family's parlor, she reported one emergency already underway. Last night she had been called at home by Mrs. Paulette Tasarz, a PTA officer. Mrs. Tasarz said a school bus driver had been drunk yesterday while driving pupils in an after-school bus. Fortunately, there had been no drastic accident. However, the pupils' trip had been delayed over an hour by the incident. Several parents had been informed of the episode, and were understandably upset. Mrs. Culverwell had planned to spend part of the day settling the questions raised by the event.

Mrs. Culverwell's suburban home had convenient access to an expressway that ran near the school, and the drive was relatively brief. We arrived at Reilly at 8:12.

ENTERING THE OFFICE

As we entered the school office, Mrs. Lange, a first grade teacher who had arrived early, came over to consult with the principal about a proposed in-class performance. Mrs. Lange had recruited a female Polish professional singer and entertainer who was travelling in the United States. She performed Polish songs especially for children. Mrs. Lange had arranged for this artist to perform next Monday, gratis, for her class (which had a number of Polish students). Mrs. Lange wanted to clear her plan with Mrs. Culverwell, and get suggestions about how other Polish students in the school could be allowed to attend.

Mrs. Culverwell responded enthusiastically. She suggested that a note be attached to the school calendar—posted in the office, and read daily by all teachers. Individual teachers could then choose to make the performance available to their pupils.

Miss Swiatek and Mrs. Culverwell then engaged in a discussion about school security. In the last few days, two teachers' purses had been stolen from classrooms, while pupils were out and the teachers away from their rooms, e.g., between 8:30 and 9:00, before classes.

The thief (thieves?) had not been identified. However, there was suspicion that someone—a pupil?—was sneaking into the building before classes, and committing the crimes.

Mrs. Culverwell and Miss Swiatek agreed to issue an updated warning to teachers about securing their possessions. But the incident also implied that entry into the building needed better monitoring. They talked over how and where existing precautions were inadequate, and how they could be improved. They particularly recognized that the preschool opened at 8:30—before regular classes began. Some parents of preschool pupils, especially the Polish parents, were prone to accompany their children to the doors of the classrooms.

This solicitude increased the proportion of nonpupils in the school, and heightened the problems of access control; hall monitors did not know whether visitors were actual "outsiders," or parents walking to and from classrooms. Furthermore, visiting parents were sometimes accompanied by their older children, also Reilly pupils. Measures were identified to tighten up the situation.

Ms. Landes, a preschool teacher, and her aide then came to Mrs. Culverwell to talk about security concerns involving parents entering the school with their children. The three of them developed a plan to diminish such entries. Mrs. Culverwell's discussion with Ms. Landes also touched on the arrangements to be made for the visit of state evaluators, due next week, and how to manage the projected meeting with preschool parents. It was now 8:34.

Mrs. Culverwell then received a phone call from a parent whose child was on the bus with the drunken driver. She listened carefully to the obviously enraged caller. At the end, she said, "Your call largely confirms what I have already heard. But it is important that I get all of the information I can. I will be following up on this throughout the day, and you will be hearing more about the matter."

Mrs. Greenwald, the school secretary, was asked to call the bus company, and get a report on the situation. She returned to say that the driver had been suspended, and that the company would contact Mrs. Culverwell later in the morning.

Mrs. Lucas was then called down to the office via the school PA system—classes had not yet begun—to take a phone call. She arrived and handled the call, from the parent of a child newly assigned to her classroom.

It was now 9:00, and the entrance bell rang. Mrs. Culverwell, as usual, stepped outside to oversee pupils entering the front hall. This entry area only served about a quarter of the school's pupils. Still, to stress the importance of discipline, she routinely surveyed such entering and leaving pupils, unless she was involved in pressing concerns.

MEETINGS

When Mrs. Culverwell stepped back to the office, she had Mrs. Greenwald ask Mrs. DePaul down. She and Mrs. Culverwell then had a conversation about textbook orders, which were Mrs. DePaul's responsibility.

A few moments later, Mrs. Vaughn arrived to meet with Mrs. Culverwell. She was the mother of a boy on the drunken driver's bus. She was obviously very upset by the incident. She reported her son had arrived home crying, due to the incident. Mrs. Culverwell listened patiently, and described the investigation in progress. At one point, Mrs. Culverwell referred to the driver as "inebriated." She quickly corrected herself—and substituted the word "drunk"—as she recognized that the latinate word clashed with Mrs. Vaughn's raw indignation.

Mrs. Vaughn had so little faith in the bus situation that she wanted her son to travel in the future via public transportation. Mrs. Culverwell said this was her right, but requested that she put her directions in writing. As she left, she stepped to the desk in the outer office, wrote such a note, and gave it to Mrs. Culverwell.

It was now 9:21, and Miss Swiatek came in with a question about the scheduling of assessment tests for pupils. The scheduling and planning of such tests were under Miss Swiatek's jurisdiction, but there were necessarily occasions for her to consult with the principal.

In the outer office, I noticed a typical scene, which Mrs. Culverwell undoubtedly saw and ignored. A pupil from Ms. Humphery's class had been afflicted with a nosebleed, and had been sent to the office. Mrs. Tamez was comforting her, and trying to decide what next step, if any, was appropriate (see photo 92).

Mrs. Culverwell then met with Mrs. Elliott, an aide who was on the bus during the incident. She had not seen her earlier in the morning, since Mrs. Elliott was unavailable until her bus arrived and her pupils were distributed. (Not all busses had aides assigned, but the bus in question carried special education pupils; such busses had aides because of the special problems that might arise.) Mrs. Elliott provided her with a detailed report. While the driver involved was apparently culpable—and had been disciplined—there was little reason to blame the school for what had occurred. There was no way to foresee the danger, and appropriate procedures had been followed.

IMPOSING DISCIPLINE

Shortly after Mrs. Elliott left, a message came over the PA, that a teacher—Mrs. X—was having difficulties with a pupil about gum chewing during class, and requested intervention. This incident requires some background.

Mrs. X was a long-term tenured teacher. She was one of the school's few poor disciplinarians. At the same time, she generated many discipline incidents. Pupils were prone either to (1) deliberately provoke her because of her incompetence, or (2) resent her, due to the humiliation her disordered measures generated. In contrast, most other teachers, whose discipline was firm and focused, received both more respect and more affection.

Prohibiting gum chewing was a basic teacher responsibility. The building and rooms were very clean. Obviously, wads of gum on the floor and desks would provide an unattractive and possibly dangerous appearance. Furthermore, gum chewing in class is a symptom of pupil disengagement, and the school is dedicated to the principle that both symptoms and basic causes of disengagement must be simultaneously treated.

Mrs. X could not firmly and simply suppress gum chewing, but blew up into ineffectual rages. To moderate such problems, Mrs. Culverwell told Mrs. X to refer all gum chewing incidents to the office for Mrs. Culverwell or Miss Swiatek to handle.

In effect, Mrs. X was an incompetent teacher. She could not effectively discipline pupils—a key requirement for maintaining control of a classroom. Other teachers frequently had to intervene to resolve discipline situations that Mrs. X had aggravated rather than solved.

I gradually realized Mrs. Culverwell was fully aware of such difficulties. Furthermore, she had little hope of changing the personality and classroom style of a mature woman with deep-set idiosyncrasies. It was also evident that Mrs. Culverwell, despite Mrs. X's notorious inadequacies, had concluded that she could not successfully press a discharge case against her.

92

One senior teacher commented to me that any discharge case against Mrs. X had already been compromised; Mrs. X had accrued many positive annual ratings in her long-term service. Furthermore, her paperwork was always in order. It was her personal relations that were destructive. My informant believed that Mrs. Culverwell—whom she generally respected—had let herself drift into a weak bargaining situation.

The policy of protecting teachers with tenure and seniority—common to most public schools—has its costs. I estimate that 30–40 percent of the significant discipline problems I heard about or saw at Reilly could be traced to the school's two inadequate teachers. These two teachers comprised about 6 percent of the teaching staff.

THE GUM CHEWERS

The gum chewer—a girl—arrived at the office. She sat down in front of Mrs. Culverwell's desk. Mrs. Culverwell coldly directed her to stand while being addressed, and asked her a series of questions about the charge. Her voice was stern. Eventually, after her questions had established a tempo, she asked the student how and where she had obtained the gum.

This was an ingenious step. It both enlarged the pursuit and put the student under pressure to involve others—under the demands of obedience, and the fear of being trapped in serious untruths. The question "Who else is involved?" also emphasized the weightiness of the violation. For Mrs. Culverwell, gum chewing—especially in Mrs. X's class—was no laughing matter.

The girl named a boy in the class as her source. Mrs. Culverwell then asked that he, too, be sent down. Undoubtedly, this tactic increased the humiliation of the guilty girl and acted to deter further violations; wrongdoing pupils would see that they might be forced to involve others, or be accused of defying an order. The boy and the girl were both brought into Mrs. Culverwell's office. When the boy reflexively sat down, she sternly told him to stand while being addressed. She then questioned the boy about his role. At first, he denied bringing the gum into school or giving it to the girl. Mrs. Culverwell responded dourly to this tale.

At that moment, Mrs. Culverwell was called to take a phone call about the bus incident. Mrs. Culverwell saw that Miss Swiatek was available to handle the chewers, and asked her to carry the matter forward. The girl was sent from Mrs. Culverwell's office and sat in the outer office. Miss Swiatek retained the boy in Mrs. Culverwell's office,

93

and had him empty his pockets (see photo 93). The material produced included several sticks of gum. She then directed the boy to bring in a letter from his mother, apologizing for his misconduct.

When Mrs. Culverwell returned to her office, Miss Swiatek reported her findings and returned the matter to Mrs. Culverwell. Mrs. Culverwell sternly rebuked the boy, both for lying, and for bringing gum into school. For the moment, Mrs. X's problems were moderated. It was now 9:52.

The two educators' tactics deserve brief attention. It is significant that they tried to heighten parent knowledge and involvement in their children's problems, e.g., through the note requirement for the boy. But I know they both felt that parental backup in discipline situations was often spotty. Indeed, probably half of their discipline problems arose among a few students who did not expect their parents to support the school. As a result, such students were emboldened to test the school's response. Thus, the faculty's punishments rarely rested solely on parental support.

In the gum situation, Mrs. Culverwell and Miss Swiatek also worked to generate humiliation and embarrassment, and coupled this with a strong shock effect—bing-bang, the punishment is over, let's get back to learning. One can imag-

ine their tactics succeeded—the girl was forced to betray the boy; the boy was trapped in a lie, and submitted to a search that disclosed his guilt; and both of them were compelled to show deference to Mrs. Culverwell and Miss Swiatek. The "simple" episode demonstrated some of the complexities of pupil discipline.

As the case wound down, my glance ran around the outer office. I noticed Mrs. Rodriguez—a bilingual teacher—sitting on a bench, and presumably awaiting a "turn." Sitting near her was the girl with the nosebleed, the girl involved in the gum incident, and another pupil on some errand.

While Mrs. Culverwell was involved in a private meeting in her office with Mrs. Harrell (a teacher), Miss Swiatek, in the outer office, was reviewing a discipline situation. It involved an upper grade girl accused of fighting near school. The student lived outside the school area, and was typically a school bus passenger. The fight occurred when she chose to walk home. Miss Swiatek believed she was the aggressor and closely questioned her about whether she should be transferred to her school of origin. "We don't want trouble-makers here!" she said firmly.

During this same period, I saw that Mrs. Greenwald put her head into Mrs. Culverwell's office, and told her a bus company supervisor would drop by at 10:30 A.M. to discuss yesterday's incident. Mrs. Greenwald also told Miss Swiatek that there had been two calls over the intercom from the substitute covering Mrs. Harrell's room (during her meeting with Mrs. Culverwell) about discipline issues. The sub was having trouble maintaining order. Miss Swiatek told Miss Greenwald to tell the sub she would be along shortly—as soon as she had settled her immediate incident about the fight.

Miss Swiatek's discussion ended inconclusively, and the student was sent back to class. Miss Swiatek then went to help the sub. Meanwhile, Mrs. Culverwell came out of the meeting, and went to the hall to help supervise lower grade pupils coming from outdoor recess.

Miss Swiatek then came over and asked Mrs. Culverwell's opinion about transferring the girl in the fight. The two of them looked up school records, and concluded they had the option to transfer in this case, due to Reilly's current heavy enrollment (see photo 94). They agreed to have Miss Swiatek carry out the transfer.

Mrs. Rodriguez finally had her patience rewarded and had a minute with Mrs. Culverwell. The school was planning to hold an assembly dedicated to a performance by the Twirlers. Mrs. Rodriguez wanted to invite to that occasion the executive from the foundation that had provided funds for the girls' uniforms. An assembly time had to be chosen that was convenient for all concerned. She and Mrs. Culverwell discussed alternatives, and then she made an invitation call to the foundation.

THE BUS COMPANY SUPERVISOR

It was now 10:35. The supervisor with the school bus company arrived for his scheduled meeting with Mrs. Culverwell. He was concerned and cooperative. Essentially, it appeared that the company's system for screening employees was only of moderate rigor—while a driver's work required responsibility, the levels of skill and pay involved were not high.

The driver had only been working a week, when the incident disclosed his serious alcohol problem. The supervisor added that he, on behalf of the company, had immediately taken the driver for lab tests (to check his alcohol levels) when he got to the scene. The results of the tests were not yet in. However, unless they showed strong no-alcohol signs, the driver would be discharged, and measures taken to try and suspend his license. Mrs. Culverwell took notes during the meeting, since she was going to file an Incident

94

Report for transmission to other administrative levels in the system. The supervisor left her office at 10:53.

Mrs. Culverwell then went to the first floor classroom of Mrs. Taff, a preschool teacher. The class was in session during her visit. The school had received a gift of a number of decorative dishes. Mrs. Culverwell thought they might be used by the pupils in Mrs. Taff's class as presents for Mother's Day. They could be accompanied by cards drawn by the pupils. Mrs. Taff was enthusiastic about the idea.

Then, Mrs. Culverwell met with Mrs. DePaul in the library, to discuss the site for the VCR player bought for the school by the PTA. She then went back to her office, returned a call from the main board office about the bus incident, and began writing out her Incident Report. Miss Swiatek was then called in, and they discussed the forthcoming school newsletter (issued monthly, and largely composed by Mrs. Culverwell) and arrangements for tomorrow's staffing.

Mrs. Greenwald then came in. She told Mrs. Culverwell she had been called to attend an unexpected meeting of the district's principals at another site at 2 P.M. that afternoon. It was now 12:11.

Mrs. Culverwell then left the front office, to perform errands to some classrooms. The errands had the dual purpose of getting specific chores completed, and enabling her to casually see what was happening around the school. Not all good or bad events in the school automatically came to her attention. Thus, she frequently found occasions to walk around and see what was going on. She once estimated to me that, on the average, she had some contact (often quite brief, like looking through the glass of the room door) with about ten classrooms each day. After fifteen years of principalling, she could tell a great deal from even a brief observation.

She first engaged in the formal observation of a teacher. The teacher was untenured, and assigned as "full-time sub." She worked daily, like permanent teachers, but lacked tenure or a contract right to her assignment. About one-third of the school's teachers had this status.

Mrs. Culverwell regarded her as marginally competent, and had her transferred to her assignment—which was less demanding than her former one—as a last chance. If she did not improve, Mrs. Culverwell had the power to assign her out of the school, and would do that. Mrs. Culverwell observed for a while, and kept notes (see photo 95). Her two aims were to provide information to spur improvement, and to build up a record to justify rejection if necessary. As she left the room, she remarked to me, "She's still not making it." I realized she had also left a copy of her critical notes with the teacher.

We then went to the third floor classroom of Ms. Josephine Nocula, one of the Polish bilingual teachers. Ms.

Nocula's class was out at another activity. After exchanging greetings, she told Ms. Nocula that she, Mrs. Culverwell, had been invited to nominate one teacher for a special award for conspicuous excellence. She would be pleased to nominate Ms. Nocula, but on one condition—would Ms. Nocula mind writing out a draft of the nomination essay? After all, she was the one most familiar with the facts involved. Ms. Nocula was pleased with the compliment. She skimmed the forms, and said she would take advantage of the opportunity.

It was now 12:43. Mrs. Culverwell had time for a brief lunch at her desk—her daily routine, typically eaten alone. She gave Mrs. Greenwald the final Incident Report to type, and held two more brief conferences before she left at 1:20 to drive to her meeting. I did not attend the meeting. She went home directly after the meeting.

As I left her office, I looked back at a small typed letter, dated June 1986, mounted in a simple frame and sitting on top of a file cabinet. It read:

> On behalf of the Reilly School PTA, I have been selected to present you with this award.
>
> It is with deep appreciation for all the good things you have done for our school that we honor you today. We feel that you, Rosemary Culverwell, are doing an outstanding job as Principal in maintaining a very well-run and highly organized school. It is also obvious to us that you are concerned not only with the welfare of the school and its academic accomplishments, but you strive to cooperate in every way to achieve a fun-filled program for the students as well.
>
> It is a true testimonial to any school when the principal and the faculty, together with the members of the PTA, serve together as a whole to accomplish their goals. This is how it should be, and we feel that this is how it is at Reilly, and we sincerely hope to continue this closeness for many years to come.
>
> Thank you for caring and for doing such an excellent job.

A BODY OF RESEARCH

The preceding narrative covers only about two-thirds of the incidents involving Mrs. Culverwell I observed during the day. However, I am sure readers get the idea. Mrs. Culverwell's days are hectic, filled with brief encounters and unexpected demands. She has to react quickly, stay poised, and see connections between many apparently disparate events.

Research has disclosed that such patterns are typical for most principals—except, perhaps, for principals of large high schools. The causes and implications of such patterns deserve some consideration.

One factor is the matter of "span of control." In schools,

principals are oftentimes the only formal supervisor on the scene. For instance, Miss Swiatek's title as "assistant principal" is only an informal designation. She is on the school's table of organization as a "guidance counsellor," and is assistant principal only by Mrs. Culverwell's designation. While she and Mrs. Culverwell work closely together, she is required to be represented by the union, and only Mrs. Culverwell can sign personnel evaluations. Mrs. Culverwell is actually the only "supervisor" of the school's fifty-five faculty and staff members.

True, the teachers are broken down into three separate grade groups, and each group meets under a coordinator. But coordinators have no formal power. They are only full-time classroom teachers. They are paid no more for their ex-

tra responsibilities. If difficulties arise in classrooms, teachers cannot easily consult with their coordinators, who are tied to their own classrooms. As a result, an enormous number of problems pass up to Mrs. Culverwell. In the end, school staff are often grossly undersupervised. The underlying reasons for this irrational pattern are complex. But, to put it summarily, an almost paranoid fear of authority afflicts too many educators.

This fear is reflected in the high levels of undersupervision prevailing in many schools—to the detriment of employees and pupils. Essentially, the undersupervision is due to the resistance of teachers' organizations, to the romantic notions of many educators, and to the primitive idea that public education tax dollars should be spent almost entirely for direct classroom expenditures—which usually means paying money to undersupervised teachers.

Each school is also largely populated by children and adolescents. Such individuals have notoriously short attention spans, and are vulnerable to adult exploitation or life-threatening mistakes. Thus, many matters that arise around a school demand quick resolution. Discipline problems, for instance, often cannot be postponed until tomorrow, or next week. Supervisors must be able to drop what they're doing, and confront and resolve emerging issues.

Parent/school contacts are also critical for a variety of reasons, but parents often don't make appointments when they come to school. If they usually have to wait to see the principal, they will be less willing to drop by.

Principals must have high energy levels, acute moral values, good interpersonal skills, determination, and the ability to keep track of many things. And, while their work environments do not encourage much reflection, they must still be relatively far-sighted, and have a vision that shapes their immediate activities.

A principal's job is obviously extremely important and difficult, but it is also rewarding. It is not surprising that many principals do not meet such demanding qualifications. As a result, many authorities believe drastic changes are needed in the whole process of recruiting, training, selecting, supervising, and compensating principals. Essentially, such changes could be characterized as "rationalization"— redesigning the personnel policies prescribed for public schools, so they are more congruent with those prevailing in most environments where people work for a living.

Chapter Eight

A BUSY APRIL

Limited–English-proficient students classified as category A and category B should not be tested with Comprehensive Mathematics Program criterion-referenced tests. These students have been identified as needing a bilingual education program where mathematics instruction is provided in the student's native language. Limited–English-proficient students classified as category C are to be tested with the criterion-referenced tests from the Comprehensive Mathematics Program.

(Item in a periodic bulletin to teachers from Mrs. Culverwell.)

APRIL turned out to be a busy month, but it began in a low-key fashion. I dropped into the teachers lounge before classes on Monday, April 14—immediately after Easter. People were casually chatting, largely about family Easter arrangements—with whom they gathered, and what was served. Since many teachers were parents of mature children, they sometimes acted as hosts, and sometimes visited married children.

THE STEERING COMMITTEE

On Friday morning, I attended the meeting of the Steering Committee, comprised of the three division coordinators, the principal, and the assistant principal. Mrs. Culverwell was out, and Miss Swiatek presided. The agenda was complex. Among other things, it covered the arrangements for standardized testing (largely developed by Miss Swiatek, but involving much coordination with others), discipline procedures for pupils who act up during recess, and particular discipline procedures for special ed pupils. Many of the committee members' asides were enlightening, and sometimes funny.

Ms. Humphery mused about whether a tendency to curse was a disability, entitling pupils to license. Then, she wondered why she was assigned the care of a particular special ed pupil when his teacher was away. "If his mom comes up here, she'll call me a nigger to my face." Despite her puzzlement, it's probable the committee members assumed she was assigned that pupil because she was adept in handling difficult discipline situations.

Mrs. Canepa, on another topic, asked whether the aides were doing their job of maintaining order in the yard during recess. "Usually, when I look out the window, I see them gathered in a group chatting, while the kids go their merry way. We'd have better order during recess if they paid more attention to their assignments."

While the points made were sometimes serious, they were accompanied by a mix of steam blowing and good humor. Miss Swiatek kept the discussion moving along, and a series of concrete proposals were developed for the minutes.

While walking in the hall, I saw a relatively common phenomenon. Miss Swiatek, as she scurried about on errands, had stopped outside a class being temporarily handled by Mrs. Z, and looked in (see photo 96). Things were OK, and she moved on. But throughout the day she kept in mind the classes that might have special problems, and she kept her eyes open.

In the gym, Mr. Phillips, the PE teacher, was conducting a series of strength and agility tests for several combined classes. One of the classes was Mrs. Lucas'. Not too surprisingly, her pupils' results in the broad jump—performed before the combined group—were not equal to those of the normal children. But even so, it was interesting to see that some of her pupils seemed pleased at the unusual activity, and the attention it generated (see photo 97). Furthermore, I did not see that the normal pupils acted unsympathetically towards the special ed pupils.

Later, I talked to Mrs. Lucas about her pupils' public testing. She remarked that, "Their motor skills are usually not as good as normal children. That's unfortunate. But they have to learn to live with that disability, and so the mixed classes are often a good idea."

When I dropped by the library, I discovered some new creations decorating the tops of the bookcases (see photo

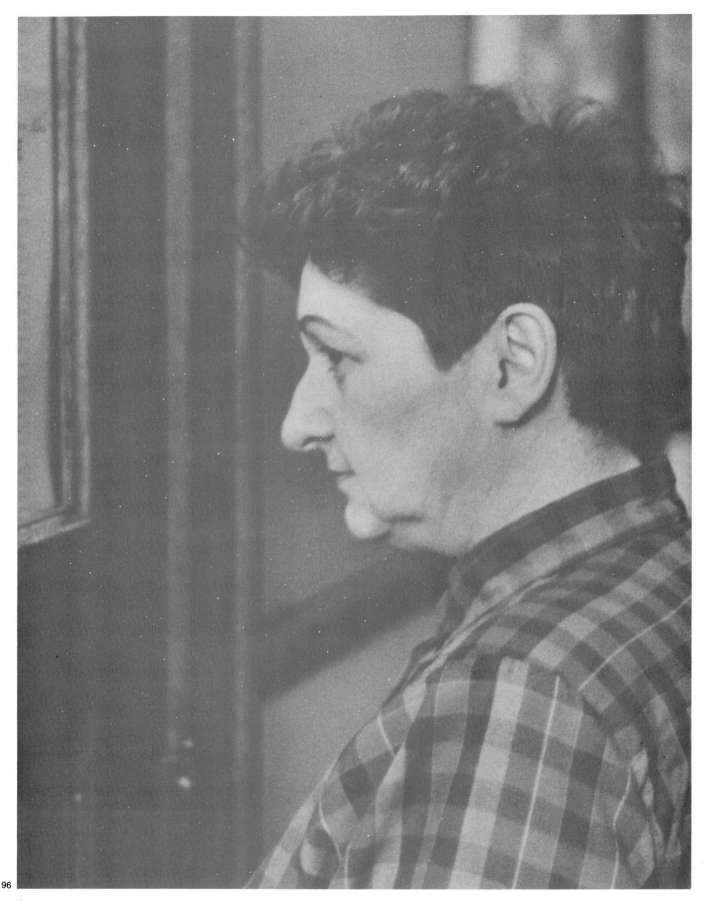

97

98). Mrs. Ebner's eighth grade pupils, for their artwork, had each manufactured and painted some form of imaginary papier-mâché animal. The creatures were ingenious and fantastic. In another part of the building, I noticed a bulletin board covered with pupils' sketches of different career possibilities (see photo 99). As the school knows, art can affect our conceptions in many ways.

In Mrs. Lange's class, the planned Polish/American concert was in progress. Her whole class, plus a number of Polish pupils from another class (and their teacher) had come for the show (see photo 100). The performers put on a lively act, and were well received.

THE PUPIL AIDES

At the end of the day, in Mrs. Estes' class, I saw one of her pupil aides (really fifth graders providing her with help during class time) hanging her pupils' newly created paintings.

The incident reminded me that Reilly relies more on pupils' help—as monitors, aides, and in other roles—than do most schools. Several motives underlie this strategy:

- Such help improves academic learning, by providing teachers with more resources and free time, so they can better plan and facilitate learning.

98

99

- The activities increase the commitment of the helping pupils to the school's objectives.
- Pupils have learning needs that extend far beyond academic skills and knowledge, and acting as helpers broadens the learning they receive.

The school's pupil involvement policies are not entirely free from controversy. It can be argued that some of the helping activities distract the helpers from formal academic learning. For instance, I asked Mrs. Estes' two female aides, who were in her class about forty-five minutes a day, why they chose to be helpers. They replied, "Being a helper is more interesting than our regular class." But part of the purpose of school is to keep pupils' attention focused on certain "uninteresting" activities.

100

The matter of potential academic losses generated by the aide system is difficult to rigorously research, but I believe the general helping process makes most Reilly pupils academically better off.

HOMEWORK

On Wednesday, April 13, I visited one of Mrs. Canepa's classes late in the morning. She agreed to cooperate with a survey of mine, and stepped into the hall. I asked each class member to estimate the amount of time he or she spent on homework on a typical day; "homework" was work actually done at home, instead of during free time at school. I chalked their options on the board, and had each of them designate their norms. The results were:

Hours	0	0–1/2	1/2–1 hour	1–1-1/2	1-1/2 +
No. of Students	1	8	11	5	1

I think the replies were honest. The students did not seem under pressure to impress me. Furthermore, on another occasion Mrs. Culverwell told me that she believes that about one hour's homework is the desirable average for upper grade students; the students' reports closely parallel her aspiration.

The one-hour average compares favorably with the real practices of many Chicago public elementary schools, and is about the average of many suburban elementary schools. In other words, it's high, but not extraordinarily high. But it is also relevant to keep in mind that typical American up-per grade elementary pupils average about two to three hours of television a night, and that Japanese pupils of the same age have about two to three hours of homework a night.

I do not believe any serious harm would come to American pupils if they had to do more homework—and consequently had less time for television and equivalent activities. Increasing the amount of well-planned homework done by pupils could be a low-cost way of increasing pupil learning. But despite the virtues of more homework, there are problems.

Right now, the Reilly teachers work fairly hard. More homework would not only mean more work for the pupils, but also for the teachers. This would be especially true if the added homework was not backed up by parental monitoring (in Japan, such monitoring is typical). And, in the case of schools like Reilly—despite instances of notable parent support—many parents do not or cannot effectively support the school. As a result, while increasing homework demands seems logical and appropriate, there are complications. Whatever response we develop to the present norms, we must recognize that many young Americans, including some Reilly pupils, are not asked to work very hard at learning.

I then visited Mrs. Lucas' class. She was reading a story to some of her pupils (see photo 101), while Mrs. Barreto worked with others at the side of the room. In her reading, Mrs. Lucas would periodically involve the pupils, asking them questions to test their comprehension.

In Mrs. Estes' class, now that the Easter Bunny was over, a new project was afoot—for Mother's Day. Mrs. Estes had brought in an enormous bag of clean cloth remnants. Her pupils were invited to choose pieces they preferred. Many of

101

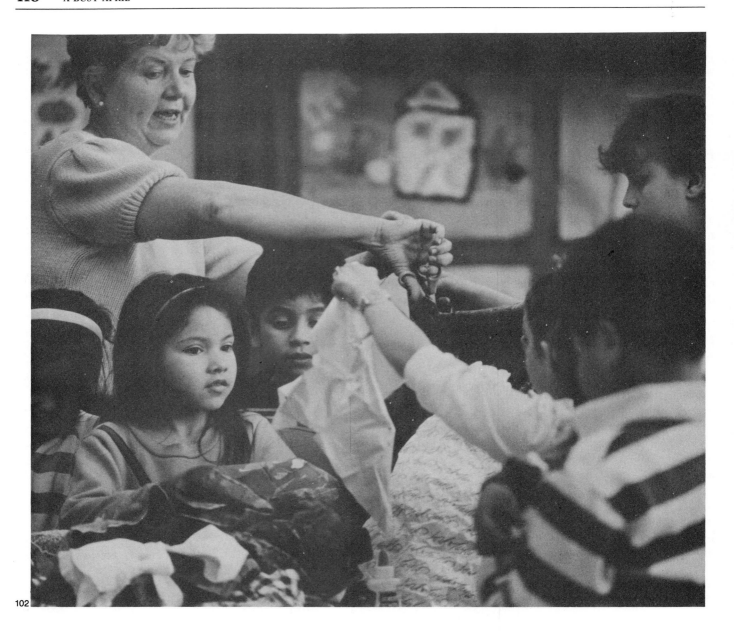

102

them were excited by the opportunity (see photo 102). After the distribution, she began working with a reading group, while her aides helped pupils cut their pieces into appropriate sizes to paste on the empty milk cartons Mrs. Estes had also brought in. The cartons, decorated with the cloth, would be used to hold artificial flowers.

FRIDAY AFTERNOON

Friday afternoon classes were often pervaded with a special spirit, anticipating the weekend of freedom. In Mrs. Windham's class on Friday afternoon, a musicale was in progress. Her pupil Jennifer Moy had brought in her cello, and was giving the class a performance, coupled with a lecture-demonstration. The students were attentive (see photo 103). It was also amusing to see the usually reserved Jennifer excitedly explain the music, and quiz the pupils as if she were a teacher.

Mrs. Canepa was leading her students through a lesson on health. They took turns reading aloud sections from their text, and she would occasionally prod them with questions. The particular topic was alcoholism. The students were moderately interested.

When I returned to Mrs. Windham's room at the end of the day, I found Jennifer performing a lovely Chopin "Valse" on the piano for the class. Meanwhile, the pupils worked on art assignments—each drawing a picture of a cello. The acoustics of the room were remarkably lively. I wondered how much the children recognized the beauty of the moment.

As I dropped by the office before leaving, I ran across the completion of another art project. It was the birthday of Mrs. Greenwald, the school secretary. One teacher had asked her pupils to draw birthday cards for her. The students were personally delivering them to Mrs. Greenwald; naturally, she was filled with gratitude.

On the next Wednesday, teachers delivered the third quarter report cards to parents. I overheard a telling exchange between Mrs. Ebner and one mother. The mother's English was evidently poor, and her level of comprehension was uncertain. Mrs. Ebner noted that, "Your son is nice, and a smart boy, but he is doing poorly in school. He should not be getting F's."

The mother seemed nonplussed by the remarks. Mrs. Ebner went on to say, "You should make it clear to him that you are upset. Do you punish him for his F's? Do you know how to punish him?" There was no clear response to this direct question.

Later in the day, I discussed this exchange with Mrs. Ebner and Miss Nicks, both of whom taught the boy. Their

mutual belief was that the mother understood Mrs. Ebner, but felt unable to control her son. Miss Nicks noted that the boy was her second son to pass through Reilly. Mrs. Ebner and Miss Nicks both said she had been obviously unable to control her first one—to make him act responsibly about school. Mrs. Ebner noted that actually, the second son was more tractable than the first. He might be restrained and corrected, but the mother's determination had apparently been sapped after losing control of her first son.

In the mid-afternoon, the teachers took a break in their report card meetings. They adjourned to a classroom, where an elaborate buffet meal had been ordered (by the social committee). A very relaxed half hour followed. The spirit of the occasion was heightened by coincidence, and by the single-sex nature of the gathering (none of the male teachers attended the buffet—partly because there were so few, and partly because even these few usually had jobs that did not permit them to work overtime to see parents). I was the only male at the gathering.

It seems that yesterday, Mrs. Canepa had noticed a male pupil reading papers concealed in a folder. She examined the materials and discovered a collection of lewd pictures. Assuming a teacher's prerogative, she confiscated the folder. To inform her peers, she brought the folder to the social,

103

and passed it around. It generated considerable amusement (see photo 104).

At the end of the buffet, the teachers returned to meet parents who could only make late visits. One visit I saw in Ms. Humphery's room provided food for thought. The family was Hispanic, and the mother spoke little if any English. Ms. Humphery asked the mother if she "understood" English, and she gave a vague assent. The conversation then was carried out via Ms. Humphery's English, plus the student-daughter's occasional translation. Some of Ms. Humphery's remarks focused on the daughter's relatively unsatisfactory performance. I was doubtful that the daughter was providing an ideal translation of this complaint.

One appreciates what was underway. The mother was ashamed to confess her near ignorance of English. Ms. Humphery wanted to display self-reliance, and avoid asking a translator to be sent up. (Even with the services of an aide-translator, Ms. Humphery might expect the discussion would be unsatisfactory.) Finally, the daughter's skills (and interest) for transmitting bad news to her mother were uncertain. And so the conference was not very productive.

As I dropped by the office before leaving, I saw Miss Swiatek engaging in a little follow-up. She had sent a memo to teachers, asking them to refer to her any parents whose children were absent over a certain number of days. She personally spoke with these parents, to see if such unusual patterns were justified. While I was present, she talked to a father who explained his daughter had been afflicted by a persisting illness.

Friday was April 29, the last school day in the month. In the afternoon, I went along as Mrs. Estes took her pupils on an excursion/adventure. They walked to a pet store to buy a gerbil for their room. Mrs. Estes and her helpers moved her pupils over several blocks with alacrity and order. Her principle was to walk them quickly, so they did not have time to stretch out. Their goal was a large neighborhood store. As Mrs. Estes knew, one of her former pupils was a clerk at the store; this assured them a warm welcome. The pupils were treated to a tour, and even allowed to pet some animals. After the tour, the gerbil was selected, purchased, and brought back to the room.

At school, another adventure was underway in the gym. A female faculty team was playing the eighth grade girls in a three-game volleyball series. The faculty team included Mrs. Canepa, Miss Nicks, and Ms. Humphery. The audience were the students and teachers from fifth grade and up. The contest generated a high level of interest (see photo 105). Part of the excitement was due to the students' ex-

104

105

quisite tension in wondering whether to cheer for their teacher or for the student team, their "natural" group.

As I left the tumultuous gym at 1:30, the faculty led in the first game, 10–5, needing twenty-one points to win. When I met Ms. Humphery during the next week, I asked the final outcome. She smiled and said, "We were kind, and finally let them win two of the three games."

CARNATIONS AND TESTS

When I entered Mrs. Estes' class on the first Monday in May, she was wearing a carnation on her blouse. I discovered the first week of May was Teacher Appreciation Week. Each day of the week, either the PTA or the Student Council carried out an act of appreciation for the teachers. As part of Teacher Appreciation Week, Mrs. Estes had a carnation delivered to her that morning before class by two members of the council, who made similar deliveries to all teachers. When I visited Mrs. Lucas' class, I saw Mrs. Barreto had been treated as one of the faculty; I am sure the recognition pleased her.

On Tuesday, I visited Ms. Humphery's class. Shortly after the Pledge, Mrs. Kane arrived with the Tuesday Teacher Appreciation gift—cupcakes, courtesy of the PTA. A moment later, Mrs. Malstrom, another teacher, arrived in the room, and a long-scheduled test got underway. I had had many contacts with the school's formal testing program, but this was my first occasion to see it operating from the beginning. The procedures were established by the board. They required that some other professional—in this case, Mrs. Malstrom—be physically present in the room, and that the classroom teacher play only a subordinate role. The object was to prevent unfair manipulation by regular teachers—occasionally done so their class's score would look good.

Ms. Humphery had the students move their seats apart, simple and clear instructions were recited, and Mrs. Malstrom passed out the question and answer sheets. The students gave serious attention to the papers and got started. Mrs. Malstrom and Ms. Humphery acted as co-monitors.

The topic of formal testing is important. In the abstract, "tests" are an essential component of all forms of learning. The term simply refers to examining learners, to see whether and how much they have learned. Without some form of test, it is impossible to imagine efficient learning occurring. We could never know whether teaching (or self-instruction) had been successful, or if it had failed.

As Mrs. Culverwell had remarked at an in-service, tests can be given in an enormous variety of ways: oral exams, written reports, physical exercises, written prose replies to questions, and various forms of the common short answer or objective tests.

Just as there are many kinds of tests, so too are test results used in a variety of ways. Learners need to know where they are succeeding or falling short. Teachers need similar information, to encourage individual learners, and to assess their own teaching. In schools, principals also need such data, both to assess individual teachers, and to estimate the overall efficacy of the school. In addition, other agencies use such data for assessment purposes: parents, both with regard to their own children and in evaluating overall schools; boards of education, which must report to the public; and, in the case of American public schools, many state education departments also have responsibilities to monitor school efficiency.

These diverse persons and agencies often need different kinds of information: individual teachers may use forms of tests almost daily, to direct their routine planning, while upper level supervisors need less frequent, more synoptic and objective information.

Mrs. Culverwell uses a variety of types of test data. She examines students' papers kept in their folders or posted in classrooms, receives stacks of pupils' arithmetic exercises, reviews report cards, observes pupils' in-class recitations, fills her office with pupils' artwork, sees and hears assembly performances, and keeps track of classroom and schoolwide test score results—with the help of Miss Swiatek and Mrs. DePaul.

In addition to the teacher-generated tests and recitations, which pupils face every day, the school has an elaborate schedule of tests required by out-of-classroom agencies, e.g., the Chicago Board of Education, or the Illinois State Department of Education. The test in Ms. Humphery's class was generated by one of these external systems. These externally imposed tests are all in objective, or short answer format so they can be scored by machines, and produce easily computerized results.

The contents of such standardized tests clearly affect school, administrator, and teacher priorities. In a rational sense, much teaching for the test occurs: subject matter that is expected to be on the tests is emphasized, and the school tries to get an idea of the materials to be covered on tests. The term "teaching for the test" is usually seen as pejorative. However, that interpretation is often simplistic. Someone needs to decide what should be taught in classrooms, and that decision should not be left to the haphazard authority of thousands of individual teachers. Standardized tests are a way of establishing collective responsibility for such decisions about priorities.

Despite the strong case that can be made for objective tests as a monitoring tool, they also have real deficiencies. Obviously, "teaching for the test" can be conducted in a simplistic way—especially if a test is poorly designed. Furthermore, technically speaking, the connection between particular established tests and the curriculums they are supposed to monitor is not always good—and is sometimes quite poor. In other words, students may have really learned the material prescribed and taught, but still score poorly due to an ill-designed test.

Reliance on objective tests may also overstress the importance of certain subject areas, and of limited forms of measurement and learning. Some of these tensions were evident in Reilly. Mrs. Culverwell obviously wants her teachers to pay careful attention to objective test results. At the same time, both she and the staff are dedicated to attaining innumerable other learning goals unrelated to such tests—having pupils learn obedience, diligence, art, singing, loyalty, politeness, and good humor. Indeed, in Mrs. Canepa's class, even the board's curriculum stresses matters such as public speaking and interpretive reading.

It seems that, at Reilly, due to some mix of determination and ingenuity, the broad and narrow goals of education are simultaneously pursued with efficiency. Unfortunately, in too many schools, this balancing act either tips towards foolish ignorance of objective tests (or tests of any form), or excessive pursuit of high test scores.

IN CLASSROOMS

On the morning of Wednesday, May 11, I attended the meeting of the Language Arts Committee. It included Mrs. Canepa; Miss Knott, the librarian; and Miss Bressler, a Learning Disabilities teacher. Each committee was obligated to generate an end-of-the year written evaluation of its work, and Miss Knott, the chair, directed their attention towards this topic. There was also discussion of the pending Balloon Day. On that day—June 2—each pupil releases a helium-filled balloon containing a note written by the pupil in an elaborate celebration in the schoolyard. The notes invited balloon finders to write an acknowledgement back to the school. Balloon Day was under the jurisdiction of the committee, and particularly concerned Miss Bressler.

In the gym, I saw two classes (one of them Mrs. Windham's) playing a game that was new for them—T ball. Mr. Phillips, the gym teacher, first explained the rules. The ball used was large and relatively soft, and the two classes were soon in hot competition.

During the middle of the day on May 12, I dropped in on Mrs. Estes. Her pupils were elsewhere, and she was cleaning with the help of her aides. Mrs. Estes noticed that one of the aides was wearing an artificial diamond ring on her ring finger. She told her, "You're not engaged. You have the ring on the wrong finger." Mrs. Estes' tone made it clear she thought the error should be corrected, and the aide cheerily made the change.

The episode reminded me of a graduate student of mine, who observed a ninth grade girl in a school wearing a "pre-engagement" ring—this is what the girl called it. Neither the grad student nor I felt the story was entirely funny. Ninth grade pupils involved in "pre-engagements" may feel licensed to try other forms of premature experimentation. Mrs. Estes' motherly act of intervention reminded me of the many ways that semi-formal teacher/pupil contacts, such as come from pupils being aides, can be of great benefit to young people.

On Friday, the next day, in Mrs. Canepa's room, just before a class started, a messenger came in with a note. It authorized Mrs. Canepa to deliver certain medication to a student with a minor ailment. As she turned the medication over to the boy, several other boys entered. They offered her casual advice about the boy's health. She responded in a friendly but quippy fashion, and it made an engaging scene (see photo 106).

A DIFFICULT TIME

Since I'd been away for a week on business, I dropped by Mrs. Culverwell, and asked what had been happening

106

to her. She reported that she had been having a difficult time.

She had been prepared for a semi-final evaluation conference with a male substitute teacher who was untenured, but regularly assigned to the school. She had determined to give him an unsatisfactory rating, so he would be assigned elsewhere next year. And, from what I knew, that rating was justified. She foresaw the anticipated conference would be stormy: the teacher wanted to stay at Reilly, and did not want a bad mark on his record. She arranged for the building engineer—a husky male—to be outside her door during the meeting, in case things turned violent. In fact, the meeting was very tense, but the engineer did not have to be called in. After this, the teacher was entitled to one more evaluation visit.

When Mrs. Culverwell later went to his room for the visit, while the class was in session, she found his door locked. The locking was a deliberate act of exclusion. Rather than risk a violent confrontation, the next morning she simply arrived at his room coincident with the entry of the students, walked in with them, and completed the visit. (The teacher did not have the determination to publicly drive her from the room after she had entered.)

In concluding this story, Mrs. Culverwell told me her final private meeting with the teacher was tranquil. He was even somewhat apologetic about his prior noncooperation. She mused, "Maybe he will work out better with another principal."

Mrs. Culverwell also had a sharp conflict with Mrs. X. One of her graduating pupils had been admitted to a Chicago public high school for the performing arts. The girl was an accomplished pianist and hoped her entry would advance her career plans. But it happened that she would be receiving a low grade from Mrs. X in one subject. That grade might bar her enrollment in the prestigious school. She received the grade because she had been given a zero for one homework assignment. The zero had considerably brought her subject average down—and would earn her the low grade. The girl's mother questioned this evaluation.

According to Mrs. Culverwell, the girl had actually done the homework in a competent fashion. She had simply turned it in late, due to a misunderstanding (she was a new student in the school). Mrs. Culverwell could appreciate the lower grade for the late homework. However, it seemed unreasonable to make that grade a zero, compared to simply a failing grade. In other words, if 65 percent was passing, perhaps she should have received 60 percent—but not a zero. In a mathematically calculated grading system, one zero could drastically pull down an overall grade.

In lengthy and tense discussions with Mrs. X, Mrs. Culverwell found her unyielding. She felt that grading was her absolute prerogative. Finally, Mrs. Culverwell overruled Mrs. X, and gave the pupil the higher grade she believed she had earned. When I heard the story, I remarked to Mrs. Culverwell that she had the obligation to personally sign each report card; that signified she had the authority to finally accept or reject a teacher's conclusions; otherwise, why should she have to sign? Mrs. Culverwell recognized the responsibility inherent in her position, and pushed through principled decisions despite notable resistance.

A SMALL DRAMA

When I dropped by Mrs. Canepa's room, I observed a small drama. While the class was in session, Mark, a seventh grade student, came running into her room—immediately pursued by Mrs. X. She was screaming at him. The tenor of her remarks was that Mark had "thrown a chair" at her, and that she would "press charges." Her voice was at the loudest and shrillest pitch I had heard in the school.

Mrs. Canepa assured Mrs. X that she would follow up on the matter. Mrs. X consequently left Mark standing despondently beside Mrs. Canepa, his homeroom teacher. Eventually, I obtained the background on the situation.

During a class, some dispute had arisen between Mrs. X and some students. Eventually, Mark, in his aggravation, pushed (threw?) a chair at Mrs. X. Shocked at his own misconduct, he then ran away, and she pursued him into Mrs. Canepa's room.

From what I heard, Mark was evidently not a model student. However, it also seems likely the incident was not well handled. In any event, apparently a chair had been thrown at a teacher, and Mrs. Canepa set out to collect evidence (compared to leaving that task to Mrs. X). She interviewed several pupils (see photo 107). The best informed ones were sent to Miss Swiatek's office, to complete written statements. Mrs. X, relying partly on such evidence, did file a criminal charge against Mark. (I do not know the outcome of that charge.)

Mark's parents came in at the school's request. They generally defended his conduct. They said they would enroll him in another public school next fall. For the rest of the year, it was agreed that Mark would not attend Mrs. X's class. Mrs. Canepa observed to me that it was not a bad idea for Mark to transfer to another school, but his parents should have acted in such an assertive manner earlier; they had given him too much room while he drifted on the edge of disorder.

As I walked towards Ms. Humphery's class, I discovered her outside the class door, talking firmly and clearly to one boy. She said things such as "Look at the trouble you're causing your mother . . . Other people won't tolerate such conduct . . . Aren't you ashamed of what you've done?" The pupil took her remarks very seriously.

107

As I later found out, the boy, one of Ms. Humphery's pupils, had been truant for several days. He had developed an ingenious scam. He would miss his scheduled school bus. Then, as required, he would go to his neighborhood school, and have them report his situation to Reilly. In a sense, he was "accounted" for. After the call, the other school sent him to a classroom for a day's irregular schoolwork. He would exit the school office and—instead of going to the classroom—go onto the streets for the day.

Eventually, the scam was discovered. As Ms. Humphery emphasized during her confrontation, the matter was especially troubling because the boy's mother had just taken a job. She was not at home during the day (or after school) to closely monitor him. Also, his mother could not speak En-

glish, and so her son was able to manipulate the information she received. Street life during the school day could be risky for a young boy in Chicago, and Ms. Humphery saw the situation as dangerous. She was determined to communicate this urgency to her pupil, and change his conduct. Furthermore, she knew some other Reilly pupils had been detected using the same trick, and had been picked up by the police. Thus, her tactics also were aimed at deterring others.

This is a good point to offer some remarks on the important topic of discipline at Reilly—and on the general issue of discipline in America's schools.

Discipline at Reilly seemed fine. I never saw two pupils fighting. I never heard threatening language, and few vulgar words. There was little or no graffiti in and around the school. The pupils in general were orderly and friendly. Usually, the "bad" things I saw were pupils occasionally appearing uninterested during class, or passing notes or talking when the teacher wasn't looking. And, once or twice, with significantly "weak" teachers, I did see moderate disruption, or disobedience—essentially horseplay in disregard of a teacher's directions.

But the more able teachers had a much finer sense of discipline than I had. They were sensitive to "provocations" that I often missed—unfriendly glances, disruptive whispers, concealed gum chewing. Sometimes they ignored such incidents, and sometimes they responded vigorously—especially when they believed the perpetrator was testing some boundary, or the class needed an example. They believed that such trends toward disorder should be nipped in the bud, before they festered, or other students shared the temptations.

Beyond visible disruption, a number of incidents of disorder occurred that were reported to me. I heard of two knife-in-the-school incidents and the "chair-throwing" episode, graffiti were discovered once or twice, there were several fights between pupils, and we have just heard about truancy. Certainly I did not hear of all reported incidents, and surely other incidents occurred which never came to adult attention at all.

Regardless of the actual levels of disorder in Reilly—and I believe they are relatively low, especially considering the neighborhood—it is certain that maintaining discipline is a demanding responsibility for the teachers and Mrs. Culverwell. None of them believe good discipline "just happens." They are not disciples of Rousseau. They know it takes much hard work, attention, and skill. They are also sure that discipline is intimately related to pupil/teacher/parent goodwill—as well as suppression. Readers have already observed many instances of such goodwill throughout this text.

This professional judgment about the priority of discipline is backed up by widespread public opinion. Over nineteen years, in annual national Gallup Polls on education issues, the public has rated discipline the top problem confronting schools sixteen times. In two of the three other polls, the top problem was pupil drug use—surely a form of indiscipline.

In effect, most Americans, like the Reilly faculty, believe that maintaining pupil discipline is very important—even if it involves hard work for adults. Furthermore, most Americans do not believe schools are now doing a good job at discipline. I agree with this popular conclusion, despite the fine level of discipline at Reilly. Considerable data show that the long-term trends have been for increases in the number of disordered acts by young Americans, e.g., juvenile arrests, drug use, and sexual experimentation. There have

been some recent improvements in such distressing trends. However, we still have a long way to go to attain the levels of order typical of thirty or so years ago.

There are innumerable causes for this pattern of increased youth disorder. But one cause is particularly relevant here. It is the general lack of sympathy that one would find among American intellectuals—or education researchers—for the discipline policies applied at Reilly. At Reilly, teachers carefully monitor pupil conduct; give a high priority to maintaining order; where necessary use shouting, public embarrassment, and police involvement for deterrence and punishment; and often assume that small acts of indiscipline may lead to serious disorder. The principal fully supports such policies.

When pupils persist in indiscipline, the school solicits parent support, and is grateful for such help. And, where poor at-home discipline aggravates the problem, the faculty try and cajole and harass parents to change.

The teachers believe such measures are justified because some—not many, but still too many—Reilly pupils end up in deep trouble. Getting them to change may be a life-or-death issue. I ran into Miss Swiatek just before her meeting with a parent. She remarked that the mother was distressed: her thirteen year old daughter had left home, and was living with some girl friends. Miss Swiatek mused as to whether the daughter was supporting herself by prostitution: how else could the girl help maintain an apartment with two girl friends?

The Reilly discipline policies are not always successful. But they work relatively well, and reveal the school has a high sense of commitment and realism. No one can accuse the faculty of giving up easily.

IN CLASSROOMS

When I visited the school on Monday, May 23, my first stop was Mrs. Estes' room. She mentioned to me that something special had happened recently to Julio, one of her pupils. She asked him to explain. He said his birthday had been on Saturday, and that Mrs. Estes had dropped by. As the class continued, she noticed that one boy had done unusually well in writing out and illustrating his story for the day. She had him go around the class, showing his good work to other pupils. She knew many ways to make each child feel special. It was also amusing to see the device she and other early grade teachers used to make sure pupils delivered records to pullout teachers: the notes were pinned on the pupils' backs (see photo 108).

The next day, in the schoolyard, I realized I was becoming familiar with students—especially their pairing tendencies. I noticed Mrs. Estes' two aides hanging out together, and also

109

two close friends from Ms. Humphery's room. And then, with the fine weather, baseball card trading revived among the boys (see photo 109). Eighth grade pupils began to wear one harbinger of graduation—their graduation ribbons. Eighth graders received these ribbons (which they immediately began to wear around school) as graduation day approached—if they met certain academic standards. If they did not meet the standards, they would not get their ribbons until just before graduation. About 40 percent of the students received their ribbons early.

On Wednesday, before classes, I attended a meeting of the Graduation Committee. It was comprised of five teachers, most of whom regularly dealt with the eighth graders involved. The committee had to plan the public occasions associated with graduation: "final" graduation, robes and all, done before parents; "practice" graduation in dress clothes (minus robes), done before all of the students the day before graduation; a party and dance after practice graduation; and a brief social after final graduation. The structure of these occasions was largely set by existing tradition, and the PTA also accepted responsibility for the dance-party after the practice. Thus, the committee did not have to create everything from scratch. But there were still decisions to be made.

The prime issue at the meeting might be characterized as *E Pluribus Unum*—from many, one. The school was comprised of many ethnic groups—white, black, Polish, and Spanish. These groups could even be further subdivided, e.g., Puerto Rican, Mexican-American. The teachers thought the entertainments presented by the graduates—choral songs, recitations, and speeches—should represent such diversity, and concurrently recognize the students' basic commonality as Americans. The committee discussed how to represent those complex themes. Different persons might reach different conclusions as to the appropriate balance; but there was no doubt the committee members were wrestling with an important aesthetic challenge: designing a serious rite (see photo 110).

THE CINCINNATI TRIP

On the morning of Friday, May 27, I attended a before-class meeting of some pupils and Mrs. Canepa and Miss Nicks (see photo 111). The meeting was a briefing for the members of the graduating class who, next Friday, were going on a two-day overnight trip to Cincinnati. They would be chaperoned by the two teachers, plus a former Reilly

110

111

112

male teacher who would also come along. The chartered bus would leave Friday and return Sunday evening. About half the graduates—twenty-five pupils—chose to go on the "for fun" trip, featuring two visits to a large amusement park. The $140 trip costs were paid by each pupil and his/her family. It included bus fare, two nights at a motel, meals, and amusement park admission. The teachers' costs were covered by the students' charges.

The teachers emphasized that the trip was not sponsored by the board, but the parents. The board bore no responsibility for any mishaps that might occur (and, implicitly, all responsibility rested on the teachers).

They outlined the trip rules. At the amusement park, students would reassemble every three hours. If any student(s) was late, the others would wait until the whole group assembled. At the motel, one of two policies would always be in effect: either all pupils' room doors would be open, or all would be closed. There would be no half and half. Pupils were encouraged to stay off their phones, since their parents

might call them; furthermore, the teachers reserved the right to suddenly visit any room. They would try to call ahead if they exercised that right—but if the phone was busy, they would barge in without warning. It was also stressed that any disorder would not only affect the group itself, but future graduating classes, which might be denied motel reservations because of the school's damaged reputation. The teachers' realistic, clear statements were typical of the Reilly approach to such occasions: have fun, but stay within bounds. The briefing was supplemented by written instructions for pupils and their parents.

As classes began, I visited Mrs. Estes. The class was in readiness for the coming final music assembly, to take place later that morning. The students—dressed in their best— were having a last rehearsal (see photo 112). Meanwhile, one father—at school for the assembly—looked in through the open class door. He was responding to a powerful parental instinct: the desire to see one's child do well in a public display.

Chapter Nine

NO MORE
FIRST GRADE!

I think Tammy Morro should get the American Legion Award because Tammy has good grades, represents the school in the Math Club, Student Council President, Monitor, Tammy has responsibility to get things in order like for example cheerleader she has to teach them all the cheers for assemblies and Tammy gets along with a lot of people. She's always willing to help.

(Eighth grader's written rationale for her choice of citizenship award winner)

MRS. Estes made an announcement on behalf of her class as I visited her one day in early June. The class had stopped using double lines for their writing assignments. That double space stuff was only for first graders! Her pupils were now ready for second grade work. And so they were now writing on single lines. At her invitation, her pupils stood up holding papers displaying their new skills. This charming incident typified much of the spirit pervading the school throughout the month.

RACIAL TENSION

On Thursday morning, June 2, I attended the primary grades meeting. Towards the end of the meeting, Mrs. Culverwell came by to report on several matters and invite the teachers' comments. One item seemed especially significant. Mrs. Culverwell had witnessed an incident where a white teacher had addressed a race-tinged criticism towards a black teacher. She also was conscious that there was some tendency for social ties among faculty to go along racial lines. She wondered what these events implied about race relations in the school, and had solicited the comments of several persons—even though the black teacher involved in the possible affront had not uttered any complaint. The teachers at the meeting discussed the matter.

The most vigorous response came from the primary coordinator, Mrs. Lange, who was black. She observed that several members of the group had been impatient towards her, and she always knew they were anti-black. The remark provoked the good-humored joking it was aimed to stimulate. It became evident that the committee did not believe race relations were an issue in the school. Black-white tensions, if they existed, were only part of the normal differences among all members of complex organizations. As for Mrs. Culverwell's concerns about racial groups, such groupings were more the product of car pools, and other social patterns generated by racially segregated neighborhoods—a notorious Chicago phenomenon. Finally, they all recognized there were also many cross-race social and professional groupings.

I later discovered that the black teacher affected by the possible affront was Ms. Humphery—no pushover, she. When I asked, she told me that she had disregarded the remark, and never mentioned it to anyone. She had interpreted it as, at worst, an overstated joke. Nothing to carry further. Mrs. Culverwell launched the "investigation" strictly on her own, and when she saw things were fine, she let the matter drop.

To my mind, one other reason for the school's comparatively good racial and ethnic relations—both among staff and pupils—was the task-centered nature of the environment. People were kept under pressure to be productive. If ethnic or racial groupings became too strong, it would interfere with such efficiency.

After classes began, I visited Miss Nick's eighth grade class. She had agreed to leave me alone with them, to ask them questions as a group. I had chosen the eighth grade students since they had the longest experience in the school. I concentrated my questions mostly on the students—about half of the class—who had transferred into Reilly from other public schools. Their experience allowed them to compare Reilly with different schools. We evolved a consensus about the unique features of Reilly:

- The teachers are "strict"—they enforce discipline.
- The teachers help you study, get information into your heads, and make you do homework on time.

- The school and grounds are clean.
- There are many engaging "activities" — parties, recess, assemblies, special occasions.

These opinions generally concurred with my own observations. The opinions seemed to me to be a strong justification for the policies applied in Reilly: work pupils hard, make them be obedient, and encourage them to have responsible fun. To apply such policies to students, the faculty must also work hard, be obedient, and have fun among themselves. Unfortunately, these things often don't happen in public schools.

I also asked the students about potential improvements. Some of their suggestions were frivolous, others impracticable due to lack of resources, but some were significant:

- even more activities
- keep the school even cleaner
- more dress-up assemblies, e.g., wearing ties, jackets, dresses
- newer curriculum materials and more computers
- lockers for storing textbooks and jackets

BALLOON DAY

On Balloon Day, Miss Bressler — with the help of some students — was carrying out the "gas up" process in the auditorium. Since the helium-filled balloons would fly to the ceiling if released, there was some challenge. By the time I visited Mrs. Estes' room at noon, each pupil had received a filled balloon, and had tied it — with some help — to his or her wrist. They kept at their classwork, and waited for the moment to go outside for release. When the whole school went outside at 1:00 for release, I found it is not practicable to get 700 children to release their balloons simultaneously. It would take more drill time than the matter was worth. But the moment of release was still lively and good humored (see photo 113). As the balloons drifted up and away, Mrs. Culverwell remarked, "The last two years, they all flew north. Today, they are going southwest." Obviously, the event absorbed her interest.

When I arrived in the afternoon on Friday, June 3, pupils in Ms. Humphery's class were standing at the board, each doing a multidigit arithmetic problem that he or she had designed. The pupils were pleased to display their acquired knowledge, and also took turns critiquing each other with relative good humor.

Mrs. Estes was working with some pupils in her reading group corner. A question had arisen about the pronunciation of a word, and she invited each pupil to whisper the word in her ear — secretly. When this exercise was over, she allowed all interested pupils to raise their hands, and ask to publicly recite the correct answer. The pupils jumped with excitement in hope of being recognized (see photo 114).

114

This was also the day when the eighth graders went on their Cincinnati trip. In Mrs. Canepa's room, an incident occurred. Mrs. Canepa discovered one of the boys slated to go on the trip had deliberately struck a girl (also scheduled for the trip) during the last hour. She determined that the blow—despite some mild provocation—was in no way justified. At class changing time, she took the boy out into the hall and, with the girl standing by, sailed into him. "How would you like it if I hit you in the face if I was mad at you? Do you think such conduct by me would be justified? Do you think I will let someone come on a weekend with me who believes such violence is right?"

She insisted he immediately deliver a full apology to the girl. The apology was forthcoming. Without it, I am sure Mrs. Canepa would have pulled him from the trip.

I found the incident very affecting. Mrs. Canepa knew that such episodes might arise around the bus trip. Or, to put it another way, the natural problems of school discipline would be complicated by an overnight trip. Furthermore, on the trip, the teachers were on their own—they would not be backed up by the board if something went seriously wrong. But Mrs. Canepa and Miss Nicks—and, to some degree, Mrs. Culverwell—went ahead because they believed the experience was good for the pupils.

On Monday morning, I asked Mrs. Canepa about the Cincinnati trip, which had ended the previous night. She said there was no trouble from the boy and girl who had quarreled before the trip. However, there was one incident. As they were about to leave Cincinnati, a student had reported to her (in secret), that some students had stolen towels and wake-up alarms from their motel rooms. Mrs. Canepa thanked him, and then announced to the whole group, "I understand that some things have been stolen. I want those things placed here on my bus seat before we leave. If not, we will hold up the whole exit, and search all rooms before we go to see what is missing. The search will shorten our dinner break on the way home. Furthermore, if the stolen things are not found, the school will not be able to use this motel next year."

One of the thieves then privately came to her, confessed, and surrendered his goods. The rest of the materials (from another student/thief) were anonymously placed on her bus seat. She said the rest of the trip was fine, and the incident was no great matter.

ACTIVITIES

When I arrived on Tuesday, the Reilly Twirlers were about to put on their show in the auditorium. An officer of the Oppenheimer Foundation (which had supplied the Twirlers with a grant for uniforms) was present, as well as Mrs. Rodriguez's own parents, and a television crew from a Spanish language station. Presumably, the station had sent the crew due to the initiative of Mrs. Rodriguez. When I saw some of the Twirlers in the hall, they were exuberant about the show. I later heard that the show made the evening news.

On Thursday, in Mrs. Lucas' room, I found her excited about her discovery of styrofoam apple crate dividers. Each divider was comprised of about twenty small, bowl-shaped containers. Mrs. Lucas found that the containers made ideal holders for watercolor paints, and so she set the class to an elaborate painting project. For "canvas," they had long strips of computer paper stretched on the floor (see photo 115). Each time an adult came by the open classroom door, they were warmly invited to witness the ambitious enterprise.

In Mrs. Canepa's room, I noticed a copy of E. D. Hirsch's popular and controversial book, *Cultural Literacy*, on her desk (see photo 116). This stimulated me to reflect on how new ideas and information about education—such as the book—came into the school. The process was complex and serendipitous.

There were many information channels:

- The twice-monthly in-services often included invited speakers or speakers who solicited their invitations.
- A variety of bulletins and directives were received from the Board of Education.
- There were reports in the media about education developments.
- Sometimes articles of professional interest came to faculty attention, and sometimes Mrs. Culverwell duplicated and circulated articles that caught her eye.
- Some of the teachers were taking graduate courses, which might provide them with new and useful information. However, not many faculty were so enrolled: most of them, as senior teachers, had accrued near the maximum graduate credits for which they earned pay increases.

As a professor, I am in the business of screening new information about education, and even developing such information in my writings. It seems to me that the quality of the information about education received at Reilly was at best mixed. This is understandable. There is a lot of static out there, and the faculty often lacks the time and energy to engage in careful screening.

There is no simple solution to the problem of getting more and better information about how to improve education into schools. It is also striking (or reassuring) that many of the more important practices in Reilly—strict discipline, teachers making pupils work hard, holding lots of activities—are not matters given great prominence in much recent education literature. And so many of the school's best policies have evolved in spite of—and not because of—the information generally in formal circulation.

115

116

GRADUATION PREPARATIONS

I was out of town for a while, and next returned to school on Monday, June 20. Graduation preparations were underway. In the auditorium, Mrs. Gartner was helping rehearse some graduating pupils in one of their songs. Mrs. Culverwell was seated at her desk, filling in names and her signature on diplomas. She incidentally mentioned that, after becoming a principal, she had taken a course in calligraphy.

When I arrived next morning, I passed two eighth graders, engaged in what would be a spreading ritual—signing each other's autograph books (see photo 117).

I then participated in another form of memorializing—taking a picture of the school's attendance banner, and the Attendance Committee (see photo 118). Note that the committee's members include Mrs. Estes and Miss Swiatek. For the second year in a row, the school had won—and thus retired—the district's attendance trophy. The committee was elated. They had attained top attendance five out of the eight months of the contest.

The contest provides educators with an example of successful manipulation of pupils' group conduct: it is no accident that Reilly won the contest; they set out to win, made a plan, and carried it out. The plan involved:

- talking about the importance of attendance
- collecting careful information about levels of individual pupil, class, and schoolwide attendance
- widely publicizing such information, particularly in comparative frameworks (e.g., comparing the attendance rates of different pupils, different classes, and Reilly compared to other schools)
- having periodic—monthly and annual—recognitions for pupils and classes doing well

But, if adults can shape student conduct by such deliberate policies, it is evident that other—even more important—forms of pupil conduct are also capable of being shaped by group contests. It is a matter of adult planning and determination.

When I looked at the PTA bulletin board, I saw another graduation reminder, the PTA's farewell to graduates (see photo 119).

As I walked through the school, I ran across Mrs. Kane, the PTA president. We began to chat, but quickly ran into a mini-controversy. Mrs. Kane's eighth grade daughter came over to her, and said Miss Swiatek had told her she would be kept from classes for the day because she was wearing shorts to school—unless her parents brought in suitable

117

118

clothing. Mrs. Kane, who often dressed quite casually, remarked she was busy, and hadn't time to go for other clothes for her daughter. She might be able to talk with Miss Swiatek, but she doubted she could change her mind. After her daughter left, Mrs. Kane shared with me her strong admiration of Miss Swiatek, plus her sympathy for her very responsible daughter. Later in the day, as I walked by Miss Swiatek's office, with its door open, I saw the resolution of the controversy: a half dozen eighth grade girls, all dressed in shorts, were spending the day in her office—unless their parents later brought in suitable clothes.

True, the days were warm. But the sudden outburst of shorts was not purely coincidence. It was part of the pre-graduation testing process. If Miss Swiatek was pressed to justify her policy, she would say that several elaborate in-school occasions are still ahead for graduates. It was important they display discipline and obedience at such events. Otherwise, the occasions would fall apart, or the school would not dare hold them. Thus, control by adults must be maintained until the end, or only released after deliberate decisions. Retaining restrictions on student dress was one way of communicating such messages.

By this date, Mrs. Culverwell was involved in completing her evaluations of her faculty. In fact, those evaluations have

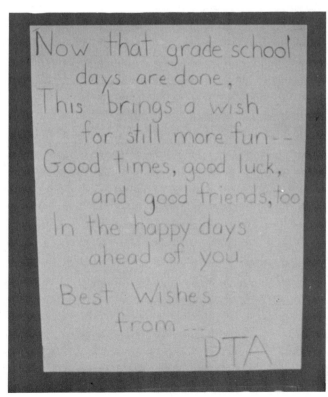

119

been developing throughout the year, with her classroom visits, and many other semi-evaluative contacts with staff. And so the final signing of the evaluations was somewhat pro forma: there should be no surprises. She rated eighteen of her teachers as superior—the highest rating—ten as excellent, and two as satisfactory. Two of her full-time substitutes were "unsatisfactory," and will not return.

Mrs. Culverwell is probably not really "satisfied" with her two "satisfactory" tenured teachers. But she did not believe she had any worthwhile options. She was not optimistic about seriously changing the conduct of such veteran employees, though she continued to try. She could, if it was essential, get certain tenured teachers transferred from Reilly to other Chicago public schools. However, in exchange for that "favor," she would probably have to take some other school's marginal teacher(s). She was not sure the trade would be worth it.

I then invited her comments on the overall year. She remarked that she would not receive schoolwide school test scores from the board until the fall. Thus, she could only have general impressions about that matter. She was quite pleased with the teacher stability throughout the year—only one of her regular teachers had left. She believes such stability is very desirable for children. The school's pupil and teacher attendance were fine compared to other schools, but still frustratingly low—presumably partly due to the disruption caused by the strike. But, rather than largely considering the past, she was more interested in using understanding of the past to shape the future—and so she launched into a discussion of improvements for next year.

In Mrs. Canepa's room, there was some license for pre-graduation hi-jinks. Some of the graduating pupils were wearing T-shirts, and inviting their friends to write slogans and other graffiti on them. One pupil asked Mrs. Canepa for a contribution. She gladly wrote something—I don't know what—in the armpit of his shirt. The informality of the occasion was also signalled by the presence of her own three adolescent children, who were all off from their own schools, and came in with their mother to pass the time.

In the schoolyard, another end-of-the-year activity was underway: a PTA party for students who had perfect attendance. They all had an hour off for play, plus free ice cream. I was in Mrs. Estes' room when her prize winners were called out for the occasion. They grinned with anticipation, and Mrs. Estes led the class in applauding their achievement. Miss Swiatek was also invited to the party, in recognition of her leadership. She attended, proudly wearing her gift corsage.

Saturday, June 25, was a Records Day—no students were present, and teachers were engaged with meetings, cleanup, and back paperwork. It was extraordinary to have such days on Saturday. However, the meeting date was one of the adaptations worked out by the board to reorganize the school calendar, which had been put in disarray by the strike. I used some of the free time created by the occasion to retrospectively interview my five teachers: "How has the year looked to you?"

THE REPLIES

Ms. Humphery was very pleased.

"My students' levels of responsibility have improved. They were able to keep discipline if I was out of the room. There were no complaints of their misconduct on the bus. No one was hurt in play during recess. Some of the students in my advanced math class were up to high school levels. Their writing ability—for example, composing made-up stories—had considerably improved. The pupils' reports in oral exercises were much better."

I asked her about test scores.

"I admit they were not entirely satisfactory; math went up about a year and a half, but reading was a little less than one year—although the range of movement was quite wide. I believe in testing, but I am unsure of the congruence between the Iowa test—the district's basic test—and the curriculum I have to teach."

Next year, she was going to take Mrs. Delgado's place as computer teacher. Mrs. Ebner—after twenty-two years in eighth grade—was going to take over her class. Ms. Humphery looked forward to the shift; it would be an adventure.

Understandably, Mrs. Lucas' retrospection was not as incisive.

"I recognize my pupils' achievements have been moderate. Still, one of them did move up to the English-speaking special education class. And I am generally pleased. The number of 'enemy' relationships has definitely been cut down. There is more of a sense of group support for each other. Mrs. Barreto's growth has been very exciting. I have never so much looked forward to coming to work as I do here. Sometimes, I feel upset to discover, 'Ah! It is the end of the day. Time to go home!' The people here are wonderful."

Next year, she hopes to work more with small groups, compared to individual teacher/pupil teaching; Mrs. Barreto could be of great help in this. She will try and give her pupils more precise advance notice of the activities that lie ahead. She concluded, "This room is my nest. We are a kind of a family here. Sometimes I wonder if I indulge my pupils. But I aim to help them get along with each other. And many of them have deep hurts inside. I have an immeasurable love for them."

Mrs. Canepa's reflections were less buoyant.

"Academically, things have gone well. My homeroom class has shown good improvement in scores. And I could claim some credit, especially for their reading. But I am not personally satisfied with my performance. I have not shown proper enthusiasm for my work. I need more intellectual stimulation. Perhaps I should consider taking additional graduate courses, and shifting my professional focus in education."

Mrs. Estes saw the matter in very bittersweet tones.

"By the end of a school year, I almost feel as if the pupils are my kids. It's not so easy to see them go up, even though it's inevitable. Reading scores have gone well, and improved about a little more than a year. Sometimes I get into so many projects that I wonder why I'm so crazy. But they generally work out. One boy, who has been moved into special ed, has especially distressed me. He has poor school skills, but is already streetwise."

I asked her what it meant to be a "streetwise" six year old. She said, "Hanging around with older kids. Knowing how to get somewhere in the neighborhood. Being able to go to a store and buy things. He is already looking for his rewards and excitement away from school. That's moving too fast."

Next year, while she would continue with phonics, she expected to get into reading stories a little faster. The pupils get excited by the stories. "We shouldn't keep them in drills too long."

Mrs. Windham, as befits a relatively new teacher, felt there were things to improve.

"The test scores were not notable; there was an average of about a .8 year increase. I should've given my better groups a little more attention. I want to better pace my instruction. The children enjoyed the field trips. I believe we should have more than two. I also moved the children and desks around too much. I've got to more clearly identify my policies, and stick by them. But it is distracting, when one realizes the home problems affecting some pupils."

I asked about the one or two pupils who had been placed to the side of the class throughout the year.

"I agree that I kept them there too long. They should be in and out. And, by the end of the year, all of them were back with the class."

I mused aloud whether she should consider adopting shouting at pupils, as a discipline device. It was common among many other Reilly teachers, who did not isolate pupils from the class for long periods of time. "After all, it may be better to quickly get things over with, compared to dragging them out."

"Do you really think I should become a shouter? I am such a quiet person."

"I know you love children. You will learn to do whatever you believe can help them."

GRADUATION DAYS

The main school agenda for Monday and Tuesday included:

- practice graduation in the auditorium before the student body (excluding the seventh grade)—almost the real thing, minus actual diplomas and robes
- a party and dance for the graduates, after practice graduation, organized by the PTA
- real graduation on Tuesday (for relatives, friends, and the seventh grade)
- reception and dismissal after graduation

These activities were organized with a definite dedication to spectacle, as can be seen in the photographs. In one shot we see graduating boys dressed up and waiting to proceed to the stage for practice graduation (both eighth grade classes were gathered into one room for this) (see photo 120). Next we see the practice procession to the stage itself (see photo 121).

120

121

122

The post-practice party for the students was a fitting end to eight long years together. The mothers prepared copious amounts of food (see photo 122), while the students enjoyed dancing and a repose from the week's hectic schedule (see photos 123 and 124). There was even a festive assault on a pinata (see photo 125).

In the midst of these activities, the more mundane life of the school carried on. I noticed Mrs. Lucas in the office, talking over the phone to the mother of a new pupil who would be coming into her class. And Miss Swiatek became involved with a complex situation about a third grade boy who found a pocketknife while with his parents at the beach. He did not inform them of the discovery, threatened a boy with the knife, and then brought the knife to school. The photo shows her quizzing one of the several boys in-

123

124

volved in the episode (see photo 126). The responsible boy and his parents eventually had to take a bus to the police station to settle the matter.

The next day was "real" graduation (see photo 127). Two students—both Student Council officers—were designated as American Legion citizenship winners (see photo 128). One winner was Mrs. Kane's daughter. Mrs. Culverwell described to the audience how the winners were selected by voting among the eighth grade pupils. I was later told that the teachers retained the right to veto that vote, but found the decision fully acceptable.

And it was then over (see photo 129). There were two more days in the year for the remaining students. These days were relatively anticlimactic, but I observed one pattern of note.

GOODBYE/HELLO/GOODBYE

The year ended on Friday, and that school day lasted only one hour. Pupils came in, received their final report cards, and said goodbye to their (former) teachers. They then were marched off to their new grades, to meet their new teachers, and say, "We'll see you in the fall!" So the occasion involved a goodbye, a hello, and another goodbye.

Some of the pupils, usually from the Polish program, came to school bearing bouquets for teachers to mark the occasion. In walking by Mrs. Lange's room, I heard (and saw) Jennifer relieving some of the tension of the hour by visiting to perform violin pieces for the class. In Mrs. Estes' room, one mother videotaped the last class. In Ms. Humphery's room, darkened to cut down the hot sun, students

126

128

129

peered excitedly at their report cards. It seemed the fare-wells in Mrs. Windham's class were especially affecting. Many of her Polish pupils brought her flowers. I was also touched by the farewells when Mrs. Grzieskiewicz brought her leaving students (from the Polish program) to Mrs. Windham, their new teacher. I felt like reassuring the students, "Don't worry, you'll be well cared for."

Mrs. Canepa had arranged to show her new pupils a videotape of an exciting roller coaster ride. After the tape ended, they were asked to immediately write a short paper, describing the emotions they might have on the ride. This paper would give Mrs. Canepa a quick check on their writing skills. Many of the pupils came from Ms. Humphery's class. They were engaged at the possibilities of this new class and teacher.

All of the students were then dismissed, and a number of the teachers went off to have a final lunch with each other. The year was over.

EPILOGUE

About a week later, I returned to Reilly to clear up some final details. A few teachers and pupils were engaged in a summer session, so the school was open. I peered into the now vacant classrooms, some with their misspelled mementoes (see photo 130).

I recalled how my introduction to Ms. Humphery really began when she shouted at a boy three feet away from her, "Ishmael, you stand up right now and apologize to this class!" I was thirty feet away, and winced.

Later, I had seen her class develop excellent deportment, and display evident good humor. I saw Ishmael conduct himself properly throughout the year, and recalled his fine presentation of an oral report. I also noticed he was academically a successful pupil, and in one year raised his reading score 1.8 years and his math 2.0 years.

Unfortunately, the year was not all success stories. Some classes—and many pupils—did not gain a year instructional in growth. And a few individual pupils, to even my unpracticed eye, were on the edge of deep trouble, despite the school's arduous efforts. Our society has not invented miraculous solutions to problems such as disintegrated families, or feckless parents who cannot shield their children from the seductive dangers of the streets. On the other hand, all of the pupils had been given a rich exposure to a benign, engaged public institution—one that asked much of them and treated them humanely. The learning generated by such an experience can be of profound—but immeasurable—long-term value.

130

Chapter Ten

INTERPRETATION AND RECOMMENDATIONS

To make a government work requires no great prudence. Settle the seat of power; teach obedience; and the work is done. To give freedom is still more easy. It is not necessary to guide; it only requires to let go the reins. But to form a FREE GOVERNMENT, that is, to temper together those opposite elements of liberty and restraint in one constant work, requires much thought, deep reflection, a sagacious, powerful, and combining mind.

Edmund Burke

RESEARCHERS have proposed that the best criteria of school quality should focus on the concept of "value added." In other words, considering the evident abilities and backgrounds of incoming pupils, how much difference has the school made in pupil learning?

Applying such criteria, some schools that are now getting their pupils to read at national norms, and motivating some of them to attend college, may be actually doing "better" jobs than prestigious schools such as the Bronx High School of Science, which takes the cream of New York City elementary school graduates, or New Trier High School, which serves an upper income suburb near Chicago. If we want to learn how to run "better" schools, we may learn more from studying institutions with high "value-added" ratings. For all the research shows, some better reputed schools may actually be "succeeding" in spite of their policies—just because certain demographic factors bring them able pupils from supportive families.

Reilly is a value-added school. Fifty-seven percent of its pupils qualify, in whole or part, for federal lunch subsidies—an index of low family income. During the 1987–88 school year, it was informed that its pupils' test scores for the previous year were slightly above the national norms.

In addition to the value-added concept, another research theme has also recently affected school evaluation. This is the "effective school" research. This research has identified the factors associated with value-added schools—the policies that these schools apply to achieve more with their pupils than other, similarly situated schools. Such research, unfortunately, often describes the policies of effective schools in rather general terms. Thus, the research says such schools emphasize "structure," whatever that means. I believe many of these effective schools have policies rather like Reilly's, but the descriptions are not precise enough to make the matter clear.

The effective school research has increased professional interest in academic competition among schools. Such competition—via publicly sponsored school recognition programs—can encourage schools to focus on relevant criteria of excellence.

Several such recognition programs are now in operation throughout America. As the Introduction mentioned, Reilly was one of a number of Chicago-area schools identified by one such program: the For Character School Recognition Program, sponsored by the University of Illinois at Chicago. The criteria developed by that program—with input from many educators and academics—placed heavy emphasis on the effective school research. Those criteria are outlined in some detail in the Schema in the Appendix.

LESSONS TO BE LEARNED

This study focuses on a particular school. There is still justification for proposing some general recommendations based on the policies prevailing at Reilly. However, as such recommendations will be partly founded on matters of opinion, readers may want to consider my qualifications recited in the brief biography at the end of this book.

My reasons for choosing to study a school like Reilly are also relevant to any recommendations derived from this study. One reason is especially pertinent: on many occasions, I have tried to propose school policies akin to those prevailing at Reilly. Many academic authorities have objected to such proposals, and have resisted my efforts to have

147

them published in the literature. The written comments of one reviewer summed up the matter: "The sort of school proposed is old fashioned. No schools now operate that way. If any schools did operate that way, it would be a bad idea."

Let me expand on those charges:

- *Old Fashioned:* It is true that, on the whole, Reilly's practices are old fashioned—in the sense that honesty, hard work, insisting on discipline, etc., are old fashioned. But that says nothing about the desirability of such patterns. Furthermore, just because a practice—such as fairness, or courtesy—once was common does not mean it cannot or should not persist in the future.
- *Not Done:* I admit that many—perhaps most—schools are not like Reilly. But there is still good news to celebrate. From my experience and research, I estimate that from 10–20 percent of the elementary and secondary schools in the Chicago area (and not just in the Chicago city system) have a tone generally similar to that of Reilly. And I have reason to believe that similar patterns prevail elsewhere in America.
- *Unsound:* By now, readers know an enormous amount about Reilly. Most of such information is not very esoteric. "You" do not need any expert to tell you whether Reilly is good or bad—you can make up your mind.

Reilly is an old fashioned school that is doing pretty well, and is not without companions. None of these companion schools are exactly like Reilly. But, by now, readers have a full feel of the central characteristics of Reilly—dedication, strictness, "activities," strong principal leadership, engagement by the faculty, delegation, etc. In carrying out these old fashioned principles, Reilly is far from alone.

These thousands of excellent schools exist in all sorts of environments—poverty-stricken ghettos, plush suburbs, stable ethnic neighborhoods. Some of them are public, and others private—usually church-related. They are somewhat more likely to be found in settled communities, but no flat generalizations are warranted.

From my contacts with practicing and aspiring educators, I estimate that 40–60 percent of them would prefer to work in schools like Reilly, or could easily be persuaded to like such schools. In other words, despite the comparative rarity of such schools, they have considerable latent professional support.

One reason for this study was to show I did not invent "my" image of a contemporary good school. That image reflects what a number of educators are now doing. The "authorities" who say such schools do not exist are wrong. These authorities have tried to hide this information from many lay Americans, and even other professionals. They do not want people to know what really works in education. Too many of such vital practices conflict with their established wisdom.

THE MOST IMPORTANT THING

The most important thing to recognize is that it is desirable and quite possible to maintain essentially old fashioned public schools in contemporary America—if the surrounding community is at least mildly sympathetic. The next thing to realize is that there are too few such schools, and too many barriers to their formation or persistence. One critical barrier is the refusal of many authorities to note the existence of such schools, or admit their apparent success.

We should recognize that not all authorities are opposed to all of the practices emphasized at Reilly. For instance, almost all the literature recognizes the importance of interstaff communication, which is strongly emphasized at Reilly. But, despite such points of congruence, many Reilly policies—especially its "old fashionedness"—are not highly regarded in the literature (except, as mentioned, in the effective school research).

The next step towards improvement is to make it possible for ordinary, competent principals to act more like Mrs. Culverwell and her other brave and effective peers—to design the principal's job so one doesn't need to be a hero (or heroine) and a genius to do it. Lessen the rigidities surrounding tenure. Provide principals with more incentives to use to shape teacher conduct. Renegotiate union contracts and revise state laws, to provide more flexibility in assigning staff. Broaden the criteria of teacher efficacy, to increase the importance of cooperative behavior towards colleagues. Allow principals to delegate more authority to associates. Give principals more control over who is hired or transferred into their buildings.

Principals need more protection and accountability—three to five year contracts, with some performance criteria specified; systems of incentive pay for principals for achievements, with significant awards (25 percent bonuses?) for meeting more demanding challenges; and realistic means of moving back to teaching (or out of education) principals who have either burned out, or consistently fail to meet goals.

Principals should be trained, selected, and promoted on the basis of broad criteria, emphasizing job-related competencies. The system should be rather like the process of training, selecting, and promoting coaches in competitive athletics.

Who would ever give great weight to a score on a written test, or courses taken, in choosing a coach for a competitive team? Successful coaches have usually trained as assistants to prominent coaches, coached lower-level teams, and eventually gotten promoted because of their conspicuous achievement.

Parent involvement is obviously important. But Reilly shows that such involvement need not emphasize formal control. Instead, subtle systems of parent/school interaction are both more flexible and powerful, and generate support and influence.

Objective tests are an important means of monitoring school and teacher efficiency. But they should not simultaneously obscure the many other educational goals of schools—discipline, pupil emotional development, and good fun in and around school.

Ceremonies, and interest in spectacle and art, are vital tools for fostering school (and community) cohesion, and can be integrated with academic programs.

Hard work and dedication by faculty and students are critical. Given this necessity, we cannot disregard the common human propensity to resist demands for great effort. Any institution that assumes that work and dedication will persist without a system of monitoring and complex incentives is seriously flawed.

NATURAL APPEAL

The key incentive that mobilizes the Reilly faculty is the powerful natural appeal working closely with children has for many adults—and most teachers. Good teachers choose their work more to perform service than to earn money. Teachers and pupils should almost have feelings of love towards each other. They should laugh and cry together. In Reilly there were many examples of such affection.

Unfortunately, in too many schools, healthy systems for bonding teachers and pupils are in decay. Faculty end up not liking their work and must strive to maintain morale. Conversely, at Reilly, things are organized to enhance pupil/teacher affection. Discipline is stressed, so people are not routinely angry and fearful. Students are encouraged to do favors for teachers. Teachers lead children in enjoyable activities and art projects. The administration backs up teachers in most disputes with pupils and parents.

Collegial ties among faculty are also important. At Reilly, Mrs. Lucas could justifiably praise the "wonderful" people around her. But in too many schools, faculty-to-faculty relationships are pervaded with withdrawal and cliquishness. Reilly suppresses these tendencies by holding frequent, varied, well-organized faculty meetings and socials. Faculty groups are also given important roles in planning school policies, and collegiality is a major criterion of performance.

The relatively recent efforts to increase federal involvement—via Congress and the courts—in school policymaking often conflict with the recommendations I have been making. The recommended changes require sensitive, close-to-the-scene micro-management, and judicious experimentation. It is hard to imagine assertive, national, broadcast policies that facilitate such approaches. Indeed, in the recent past, such broadcast approaches have been largely antithetical to flexibility and adaptability. Decisions at the state, school district, and school levels are much more sensitive to such challenges and opportunities.

True, Reilly conducts an excellent special education program, and that program was developed via a federal mandate. But many schools run poor quality special education programs—allegedly carrying out the same mandate. The key to Reilly's fine program is the school's general excellence. If all federal regulations were abolished tomorrow, the Reilly program might continue to run just as well.

Readers may note that some federal mandates are connected with grants of money, supposedly to improve school efficiency. But many of the special virtues of Reilly are unrelated to funding. Can regulations make teachers stress discipline, or stimulate a school to carefully design a graduation rite? Many other Chicago schools have as much—or more—money per pupil than Reilly, and are much "worse." Similarly, many schools would become better with less money, and more wholesome policies, unrelated to their funding. But, unfortunately, to improve things in these unwholesome schools, many people would have to work harder and more purposefully.

The proven relationship between putting more money in schools and education improvement (by all serious measures) is extremely weak, at best. One could probably generate more learning improvement throughout America "simply" by getting every pupil to do one more hour of homework daily, or tightening up study hall control (in high schools), rather than spending several billion dollars more on education. Of course, my suggestions would only generate moderate improvements. But their real defect is that they would not add one cent to educator income, or the number of jobs generated for union members. But that says something about our priorities, and how they are formed.

It would be nice to say that the merits of many Reilly policies can be determined by objective research. But while some research findings are congruent with Reilly practices—such as the positive relationship between homework and pupil learning—other important matters are more problematic. There are a myriad of policies in Reilly whose worth is hard to evaluate via research. Are assemblies good for learning? Are some good and others bad? Which ones? And how much? What are the effects of shouting at pupils? How important is art in a school program? Should Mrs. Culverwell continue to sometimes criticize staff on public and semi-public occasions? Should pupils be encouraged to bring flowers to school for teachers?

Research can provide some clues about such matters. But we will never attain certitude, and people who object strongly to particular practices will undoubtedly manage to find contrary research.

None of this is to deprecate the importance of seeking facts and statistics wherever possible. However, it reminds us that, for our lifetimes, human experience, common sense, and even that rare commodity human wisdom, should be critical components in shaping our school policies.

THE SCHEMA

THE Reilly study was guided by a schema my students and I developed over many years of school observation and interviewing. From examining hundreds of reports of interviews, I believe the Schema fairly represents the intellectual framework able educators unconsciously apply in their elaborate but tacit analyses.

The Schema outlines, in a hierarchical form, the things to be kept in mind while trying to form an effective school, or to observe a school to see if it is effective. Many of the principles involved are equally applicable to individual classrooms.

First, the Schema lists general categories, or principles. It then descends to increasingly specific and refined activities and practices. For instance, one of the Schema's three main categories is teacher supervision and support. One subcategory under this heading is a list of traits that good teachers should have. Without identifying such traits, it's hard to supervise or direct teachers. After the traits have been identified, e.g., diligence, the list then specifies observable behaviors that evince such traits, e.g., in the instance of diligence, diligent teachers come in to work regularly and on time, and carefully plan their lessons. Then, the Schema specifies ways for a principal or other supervisor to observe such behaviors, e.g., examining teacher sign-in sheets, requiring teachers to regularly file lesson plans that are examined by supervisors, observing in-class instruction for signs of good planning.

To "apply" the Schema as an observer, one simply observes what is happening through walking around, visiting classrooms, and otherwise collecting information. He or she looks, listens, reads pertinent documents, and asks questions of students, parents, teachers, and administrators. To apply the Schema as an educator, one "simply" manages school policies so the practices implicit in the Schema are put into effect in particular schools and classrooms. The text of the Schema follows. But there is one qualification: the text needs to be slightly modified, depending on the age of the pupils involved, e.g., one might not want to post an academic honor roll for students in first grade.

A SCHOOL IS A PLACE WHERE PUPILS LEARN.

1. Pupils learn to be helpful to others via words and deeds, through the practice of pro-social conduct: they learn to do good deeds.

There are many activities that encourage such conduct.

Many of the activities are formally organized: student-to-student tutoring; students acting as teacher's aides; crossing guards; hall guards; fundraising; a vital student council; service clubs; athletic and academic teams representing the school; cheerleading; dramatics, chorus, and band (entertaining others); maintenance and decoration of school and grounds; community service away from school; honor societies with service requirements; and appropriately designed and graded group projects.

Some of the activities are informally structured, but still stimulate the display of virtues such as personal courtesy, courage, solicitude, and tact.

Excellence in pro-social conduct is stimulated.

Good conduct is encouraged through positive reinforcement, either on an individual, classroom, or schoolwide basis.

- The desired forms of conduct are publicized via handbooks, speeches, the academic curricula, and teachers' and pupils' remarks.
- Good role models are provided: appropriate older students and alumni are put in contact with younger students; responsible extra-school adults come into the school and have contact with students; appropriate faculty are in touch with students in a variety of contexts; literature and history present appropriate models; ceremonies are held to honor appropriate living and dead models; and inappropriate models are excluded from the school.
- Groups that display collective character are: sent on field trips; given plaques or trophies; recognized at honors assemblies; mentioned in the school paper or yearbook; receive unique badges, pins, or jackets; have certificates placed in their files; have their photos

displayed; and are honored at banquets and in press releases.

- Individual students displaying good character are: verbally praised; communications are sent to parents; they are invited to join select clubs; and they receive some of the forms of honor provided to good groups.

- There are efficient and fair procedures for identifying excelling groups and individuals; statistics and other information are collected and evaluated.

2. Students learn to avoid anti-social conduct by learning good discipline: they learn to avoid doing bad things.

The forms of undesirable anti-social conduct are consciously identified and widely publicized.

All forms of anti-social conduct that may occur in or around the school are identified and clearly defined, and prohibited, typically in writing. Potential prohibitions might include: vandalism; cheating; fighting; stealing; carrying weapons or objects looking like weapons; using vulgar or abusive language against adults or pupils; provocative gestures or symbols; unexcused absences or tardies; leaving school without permission; wearing inappropriate clothes; smoking or possession of cigarettes; bringing chewing gum into school; inappropriate acts of sexual affinity; and possession or use of illegal substances.

Rules are regularly reviewed by faculty and administration, to see if they are up to date.

Some sorts of indiscipline are excluded through vital, tacit understanding, e.g., rudeness, lying, ingratitude, or uncleanliness.

Some rules are published on a schoolwide basis, and others are applied in particular classrooms.

Rules are widely and clearly promulgated, e.g., explained at assemblies and in individual classrooms, written copies distributed to students and parents annually, receipts signed, collected, and filed.

Clear, low-cost, speedy, and unpleasant consequences are created, made known to students, and applied against violators.

Potential violators are pursued in an even, tough, and humane manner by all faculty; and students, too, censure and report significant violations (e.g., bringing drugs into school, stealing).

Some consequence systems are formally structured, e.g., detention within one day of offense (either before or after school), in-school suspension in a tedious environment, keeping in class during recess, immediate contact with

parents when it's likely the parent can and will support the school.

Some consequence systems are more informal, e.g., voice control, "harassing" parents to make them accept their responsibilities.

Illegal conduct by pupils in and around school is automatically reported to police.

There is a simple, informal appeal available for significant penalties.

3. Pupils learn cognitive skills and knowledge, e.g., reading, writing, and arithmetic.

Varied forms of cognitive learning are encouraged.

Students should develop communication skills (reading, writing, speaking, listening, and persuasion); computational skills; analytical and creative skills; and facts and skills necessary for effective adulthood and citizenship.

Many means are used to stimulate learning.

Students are expected to work hard at learning, e.g., have significant homework (to be done at home, not largely during down time in school); instruction is reasonably fast-paced; diverse forms of tests are used to monitor pupil success in learning, e.g., standardized tests, individual and group recitations, oral and written reports, assigned interviews, and integrating class skills in extracurricular activities—being secretary to the Student Council.

Materials are presented in a well-organized fashion: teachers use lesson plans, and distribute syllabi and reading lists; imaginative techniques are often used; different methods include lectures, readings, drills, tutorials, seminars, library visits, outside speakers, mass media, well-designed team projects; occasional flexible scheduling; and there are frequent references to relationships among different disciplines.

Frequent reinforcement of learning: oral and written praise; clear, prompt, tactful explanation of pupils' mistakes; grades (perhaps even two digit, e.g., 92, or 75, compared to "A" or "C"); frequent, informative reports to parents; policies to enlist parents' help in learning; an effective and clear policy of promotion (or nonpromotion); grouping of pupils with (carefully examined) comparable abilities; public awards for intra and interclass excellence (e.g., honor rolls, certificates, honor societies, badges and pins, awards assemblies, honors banquet, and scholarships); demonstration of relevance of learning to later life (e.g., statements from visiting employers or alumni); and recognition of groups or teams of successful learners.

A SCHOOL IS A PLACE WHERE ADULTS WORK FOR A LIVING. THUS, EDUCATORS MUST BE ACCOUNTABLE, AND PRAISED OR HELPED TO IMPROVE, AND COOPERATE WITH THEIR PEERS, AND BE COMPELLED TO LEAVE IF THEY FAIL TO IMPROVE AFTER SIGNIFICANT WARNINGS.

1. Criteria of good performance are identified.

General traits are identified.

Educators should possess: the ability to cause students to learn the assigned curriculum; diligence; cooperativeness; foresight; good character; imagination; knowledge of subject matter; good humor; affection for children; and acceptance of accountability.

Teachers' traits are translated into behavioral terms.

Students display "learned" knowledge, through: test scores (appropriately "weighted" to allow for confounding variables); samples of academic work; recitations before observers; grades on report cards; or performance at next level class after promotion.

Diligence evinced via: regular and prompt attendance at work; ready acceptance of unexpected responsibilities; willingness to work extra hours; using own funds to supplement classroom materials; using all of class time for deliberate learning; belonging to (and being active in) professional societies; and reading appropriate literature.

Cooperativeness is demonstrated through: being active on school committees and extra-class projects; assisting other teachers with activities; and displaying care about the "whole" school.

Foresight is demonstrated via: well-planned lessons; and frequently bringing into class materials prepared in advance.

Good character means not engaging in conduct that will plausibly distress pupils, or distract them from constructive development, e.g., criticizing other teachers or the school before a class, dressing in a careless or unprofessional fashion, letting one's heavy smoking or drinking come to students' attention, engaging in sexual affairs or criminal activities that provoke pupils' attention.

Imagination means the ability to demonstrate new or novel (and exciting) connections between unlikely materials or topics.

Knowledge of subject matter is evinced by: a college transcript of subjects covered and grades earned; postgraduate work in appropriate areas; and demonstrated competence when questioned by knowledgeable persons.

Good humor is evinced by the teacher's response to the tensions that routinely arise in classroom and school activities.

Liking for children is evinced by the teacher's pre-teaching work and community activities (e.g., choosing to do non-teaching work with children or adolescents?), and the teacher's disposition to spend time with children in semi-structured activities in and around the school, e.g., leading some pupil club.

Acceptance of accountability means taking a supervisor's advice or attention in a nondefensive and collegial fashion, and gladly answering requests for information or explanation.

2. Desired behaviors are widely disseminated to old and new teachers, and job applicants, via handbooks, bulletins, and frequent oral explanation, either to individuals or groups.

3. Information about teachers' performance is collected by principals (and other supervisors), and generally known to other teachers and parents.

Principals know of teachers' conduct.

Organizational structures assist information gathering: staff and principal turnover are low; principal is assisted by other supervisors (i.e., assistant principal); principal has major responsibility for teacher hiring, and carefully exercises it; teachers are well trained and relatively experienced; principal does not have too many other responsibilities; principal works hard; principal has courage, experience, determination, tact, and insight.

Principals (and other supervisors) collect information about teachers' conduct.

- Formal structures are used to collect information: classroom visits (a mix of frequent, very brief unannounced visits, plus occasionally more formal visits); observing teacher/pupil contacts via glass windows in classrooms, or through open class doors, or at assemblies, or managing pupils away from class; out-of-class meetings with individual teachers or groups; collecting and examining various reports and documents (e.g., lesson plans; test scores; attendance, discipline incident, and grade records; copies of pupils' work; teacher notations on graded papers; and minutes from committee meetings).
- Informal structures assist information gathering: casual and social contacts; meetings with individual

parents or groups of parents; and casual contacts with pupils.

Teachers know of each other's conduct.

Teachers are informed about each other by: relative staff stability; gatherings for professional purposes and sociability; and carrying out some activities cooperatively.

Parents know of school activities.

Parents, individually and collectively, are actively welcome in the school, and accept such invitations.

Some form of parent or community group works closely with the school staff.

The school supplies parents with effective and frequent formal and informal individual and group communication, e.g., newsletters, notes to parents, phone calls.

4. Information collected by principal is used to shape staff activities, and hiring and retention decisions.

Principals promptly give feedback observations to teachers—either praise, advice for improvement, criticisms, or warnings.

Observations can be oral or written. They are clear, accurate, and informative.

Principals can and will use their conclusions to reward teacher good conduct, and compel persistently inadequate teachers to leave the school.

Fair, but not cumbersome, appeal procedures are available for persons complaining about abuse of authority.

A SCHOOL SHOULD BE A COMMUNITY. IT SHOULD HAVE SCHOOL SPIRIT, SO ITS "INHABITANTS" CARE ABOUT ONE ANOTHER, ENJOY BEING TOGETHER, AND HAVE PRIDE IN THE WHOLE INSTITUTION.

1. The school environment is bounded, to keep outsiders out, and populated with easily identifiable community members who share important common values.

The geographic and conceptual boundaries that define the school's student and faculty population enclose a relatively coherent group of families.

The families live in a so-called "neighborhood"; or have deliberately chosen to enroll in this school with its particular emphasis; or have been screened to assure their commitment to the school's articulated principles.

The physical boundaries (especially in difficult neighborhoods) are relatively impermeable to outsiders.

The entrances and play area are secure, or carefully monitored.

The physical boundaries of the school are demarcated by significant symbols, e.g., an attractive building; bushes, fences, or walls; a clean public space.

The community's boundary is emphasized by popular common symbols, e.g., a school mascot or motto that is widely displayed on jackets, T-shirts, pins, badges; uniforms or strict dress codes.

2. The members of the school have widely shared common goals.

Overall scholastic improvement is a goal.

Statistics about overall student academic performance are collected, widely disseminated, compared to other schools, and publicized.

Success in sports and other collective activities is important.

There are a variety of such activities, e.g., the attendance contest. They are widely publicized, and scores and standings are broadcast; team spirit is stimulated; and individual and group success is recognized.

Community members entertain each other.

There are plays, choruses, orderly parties, and games.

Everyone raises funds to help the school.

The school community recognizes its responsibility to outside causes, and donates goods and services to such activities.

3. The purposes of the school community are vitally expressed.

There are symbolic expressions.

These include school flags; school colors; statues and memorial plaques; mottoes; school songs; appropriate assemblies; and other ceremonies, awards, and acts signifying collective respect for the traditions of the school.

There are literal expressions.

These include well-phrased, widely distributed written and oral statements explaining and praising important community values.

4. Pupils live in both the large school community and in smaller, stable support groups. Such "groups" may be self-contained classrooms, or (in high schools) teams, clubs, or stable, effective homerooms.

5. The school maintains a sympathetic relationship with appropriate external communities.

"Appropriate external communities" include parents, alumni, other schools, the local neighborhood, American society as a whole, and the "communities" of the past and the future, i.e., the yet-to-be-born, and the dead.

The relationship is expressed via curriculum, symbols and ceremonies (e.g., exchange of gifts, honoring particular symbols—the Pledge of Allegiance—or traditions), or exchange of visits.

THERE is a vast literature relating to schools and education. I will just list a few relevant works, supplemented with some comments. One sorting device simplifies my recommendations: much of the general literature deals with randomly selected (i.e., nonexcellent) schools, or exemplary schools serving deliberately selected populations (e.g., private schools, or magnet schools). They rarely deal with schools like Reilly: excellent schools dealing with randomly chosen populations. Thus, much of the literature is only partly relevant to the Reilly situation.

Bridges, E. M. 1986. *The Incompetent Teacher*. Philadelphia: Falmer Press. The subtitle should be, "and what can be done about him."

Brookover, W. et al. 1984. *Social Systems and Student Achievement*. New York: Prager. A good resource on the effective schools approach.

Durkheim, E. 1961. *Moral Education*. New York: The Free Press. A thirty-six year old classic, translated from the French. Highly relevant to the values prevailing at Reilly.

Grant, G. 1988. *The World We Created at Madison High*. Cambridge: Harvard University Press. A careful study of a somewhat typical, relatively mixed-up high school.

Hanson, S. L. and A. I. Ginsburgh. 1988. "Gaining Ground: Values and High School Success," *American Education Research Journal*, (25):334–365. A study finding a strong and consistent relationship between pupils' high school success and the values they display and learn in lower grades. Very relevant to the policies applied in Reilly.

Janowitz, M. 1983. *The Reconstruction of Patriotism: Education for Civic Consciousness*. Chicago: University of Chicago Press.

Klapp, O. 1969. *The Collective Search for Identity*. New York: Holt, Rinehart and Winston. Emphasizes the need for institutions like schools to help members identify with collective goals—like the Reilly attendance contest (and suggests techniques to apply).

Skinner, B. F. 1971. *Beyond Freedom and Dignity*. New York: Alfred A. Knopf. A basic work on analyzing environments.

Waller, W. 1932. *The Sociology of Teaching*. New York: Wiley. A classic which stresses the dire effects of the adult isolation that often pervades school life. Reilly has successfully struggled to overcome such isolation.

Wynne, E. A. 1985–1986. "The Great Tradition in Education: Transmitting Moral Values," *Educational Leadership*, 43:4–14. Why and how educators should stress moral values in teaching.

EDWARD A. WYNNE is a sociologist and a professor at the College of Education, University of Illinois at Chicago, since 1970. Prior to becoming an academic, he was a labor lawyer and government administrator. His research and writing have focused on how schools and other American institutions help or hinder young people in developing good character. He has written or coauthored eleven books and over 100 articles, book chapters, and monographs. One of his recent books is *Reclaiming Our Schools: A Handbook for Teaching Character, Academics, and Discipline* (Merrill/Macmillan, 1992) (with Kevin Ryan).

Much of his work has been concerned with the nearly 2,000 public and private elementary and secondary schools in the Chicago area. His graduate and undergraduate students, after receiving training, have produced 300 to 400 written reports on different individual schools. Many of the reports have run forty to fifty pages, plus extensive exhibits. The students have also produced written reports of interviews with about 150 principals. In his classes, he has worked with over 300 teachers and school administrators, and 600 prospective teachers. He also helped organize and manage the For Character School Recognition Program, sponsored by the University of Illinois at Chicago. That program examined detailed applications from over 300 different schools. Finally, he has interviewed, in his classes, approximately twenty-five principals of excellent schools.